DEVELOPING FLUENT READERS

The Essential Library of PreK–2 Literacy

Sharon Walpole and Michael C. McKenna, *Series Editors*

www.guilford.com/PK2

Supporting the literacy development of our youngest students plays a crucial role in predicting later academic achievement. Grounded in research and theory, this series provides a core collection of practical, accessible resources for every teacher, administrator, and staff developer in the early grades. Books in the series contain a wealth of lesson plans, case examples, assessment guidelines, and links to the Common Core State Standards. Issues specific to each grade—and the essential teaching and learning connections between grades—are discussed. Reproducible materials in each volume are available online for purchasers to download and print in a convenient 8½″ × 11″ size.

Reading Intervention in the Primary Grades:
A Common-Sense Guide to RTI
Heidi Anne E. Mesmer, Eric Mesmer, and Jennifer Jones

Developing Word Recognition
Latisha Hayes and Kevin Flanigan

Developing Vocabulary and Oral Language in Young Children
Rebecca D. Silverman and Anna G. Meyer

Developing Fluent Readers:
Teaching Fluency as a Foundational Skill
Melanie R. Kuhn and Lorell Levy

Developing Reading Comprehension:
Effective Instruction for All Students in PreK–2
Katherine A. Dougherty Stahl and Georgia Earnest García

Teaching Beginning Writers
David L. Coker and Kristen D. Ritchey

Developing Fluent Readers

TEACHING FLUENCY AS A FOUNDATIONAL SKILL

Melanie R. Kuhn
Lorell Levy

Series Editors' Note by
Sharon Walpole and Michael C. McKenna

THE GUILFORD PRESS
New York   London

Printed in the United States of America

This book is printed on acid-free paper.

Last digit is print number: 9   8   7   6   5   4   3   2   1

Library of Congress Cataloging-in-Publication Data is available from the publisher.

ISBN 978-1-4625-1899-9 (paper)   ISBN 978-1-4625-1919-4 (cloth)

To my husband, Jason; my son, Allen;
my mother, Emma; and the memory of my father, Raymond,
and my mentor and friend, Steven Stahl

—M. R. K.

To my husband, Phil; my children, Miles and Emma;
my father, Len; and the memory of my mother, Audrey,
my first and most steadfast teacher

—L. L.

And to all those teachers who help our students
become readers, as well as to the students themselves

About the Authors

Melanie R. Kuhn, PhD, is Associate Professor in Literacy Education at Boston University, where she teaches courses on reading methods, struggling readers, assessment, and content-area literacy instruction. She began her teaching career in the Boston public schools and has worked as a literacy coordinator for an adult education program, a clinician at an international school in England, and Associate Professor in Reading Education at Rutgers Graduate School of Education. Dr. Kuhn is coauthor or coeditor of two previous books, *Fluency in the Classroom* and *The Hows and Whys of Fluency Instruction*, along with numerous articles and chapters. Her research interests include literacy instruction for striving readers, comprehension development, vocabulary instruction, and text complexity.

Lorell Levy, EdD, is a learning disabilities teacher/consultant in the West Windsor–Plainsboro (New Jersey) School District and Adjunct Professor at Rutgers University, where she teaches courses on literacy education. Dr. Levy has presented at both national and regional conferences on topics of literacy education and special education. She is on the board of directors of several nonprofit organizations and has spent time training parents, teachers, and health care professionals in Ghana on how to work with children on the autism spectrum.

Series Editors' Note

Every author in this series brings two sets of credentials: research expertise in an area of importance and a commitment to real-life classroom work. Melanie Kuhn and Lorell Levy fit the bill! You will discern in these pages a strong conceptual understanding of what it takes to build multidimensional, comprehension-oriented reading fluency *and* how to make the authors' recommendations work in today's diverse and busy classrooms.

We have seen enormous pendulum swings in teachers' attention to oral reading fluency in the primary grades. Where once fluency was an entirely neglected part of the reading development puzzle, it became overemphasized until it was virtually an end in itself. Now, as the pendulum moves once more in the direction of lower prominence, we risk a return to "benign" neglect, potentially crippling the reading development of those children who rely on engaged in-school reading as their only route to proficiency. Fortunately, this book presents a clear and reasonable role for fluency-building activities that embrace both repeated and wide reading with support.

Kuhn and Levy take a stance that is at once empirically sound and eminently practical. We ourselves have benefited from their constant reminder that automaticity is not fluency. Fluency is more—much more. Fluency is the prosodic sensibility that both builds and demonstrates comprehension. Fluency is both a prerequisite and a product of skilled reading.

These authors take care to nest their recommendations within a differentiated grade-level literacy plan. From this perspective, shared by authors of other books in this series, they address teacher concerns about how, when, and why fluency work should be informed by assessment, and they provide easy access to tools and grouping strategies.

Kuhn and Levy do not offer recommendations in a vacuum. They couch their suggestions in real-world scenarios that will resonate with classroom teachers in the primary grades. It will be immediately evident that they appreciate the practical constraints all teachers face. At the same time, the guidance they offer is firmly grounded in research on reading development, and it reflects their support for the use of increasingly challenging texts. They demonstrate in clear and practical terms how providing instructional support can make this goal attainable.

SHARON WALPOLE, PhD
MICHAEL C. McKENNA, PhD

Acknowledgments

We thank Series Editors Sharon Walpole and Michael C. McKenna for giving us this opportunity and helping us see it through. We would also like to thank Craig Thomas, Mary Beth Anderson, and Anna Nelson of The Guilford Press for their help and support throughout the process of seeing this book to publication. Without them, this book would not have been possible.

Contents

Purchasers can download and print larger versions of selected figures
from *www.guilford.com/kuhn2-forms*.

CHAPTER 1
· · · · · · · · · · ·

Foundational Skills and Open-Ended Learning

WHEN AND WHY?

GUIDING QUESTIONS

- What is the difference between foundational and open-ended reading skills?
- Why are both foundational and open-ended reading skills important?
- When should the various skills be integrated into the literacy curriculum?
- How can challenging texts be part of literacy development from the earliest years?
- How does fluency fit within students' reading development?

This is a book on fluency, so why are we beginning with a chapter on foundational skills? We see fluency as a bridge between basic skills and open-ended learning. Like all bridges, both ends must be grounded in order for the bridge to be stable. We start, then, with the foundational skills side, which must be part of your thinking if you want to help your students consolidate skills and progress. We then discuss how broader skills can be integrated throughout a literacy curriculum that is effectively grounded in the Common Core State Standards (CCSS; Common Core State Standards Initiative, 2012).

How students read changes significantly across the primary grades; as a result, what you hear as they read aloud is likely to be very different depending on their age (e.g., Chall, 1996; McKenna & Stahl, 2009). Figure 1.1 provides a preview and shows that this developmental process is not linear. That is, the youngest learners

1

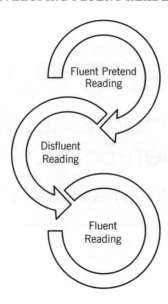

FIGURE 1.1. Reading development across the primary grades.

(PreK and kindergarten) will often "pretend" read, making up the story or information based upon either the pictures accompanying the text or what they remember from having had the book read to them previously. Because they are relying on their own language, their "reading" usually sounds fairly fluent. First graders, on the other hand, are likely to sound quite stilted. Since they are trying to figure out many—or even most—of the words, their reading loses the smoothness that existed when they had memorized, or were making up, the text. In other words, it lacks some of the essential characteristics of spoken language or skilled reading. While the words are likely to be correct, they are read in such a stilted manner that they are either unconnected to one another or produced in such awkward phrasing that the reading fails to communicate meaning. Luckily, though, by the time they reach second grade, children are likely to have a strong bank of sight words, or words they recognize automatically. They should also be starting to integrate intonation into their reading at this point. As a result, their oral reading begins to sound fluent again.

Our goal for this chapter is to discuss the ways in which the development of foundational reading skills varies across the primary grades and how instruction needs to change accordingly if we are to support students' literacy learning adequately (e.g., Hayes & Flanigan, 2014; Mesmer, Mesmer, & Jones, 2014; Walpole & McKenna, 2009). At the same time, we must attend to oral language, vocabulary, and comprehension development throughout these early years if we are to ensure students' ability to deal with complex texts (e.g., Hamilton & Schwanenflugel, 2011; Neuman & Celano, 2012) and the requirements of the CCSS (Common

Core State Standards Initiative, 2012). Ultimately, learners need to develop both foundational and broader skills if they are to be successful from the very start. To ground your thinking about foundational skills, Figure 1.2 provides a list of important terms.

Reading Development: Differing Skills at Different Stages?

All learners need access to a range of skills to become successful readers. Scott Paris (2005, 2008) describes these differing skills as constrained (e.g., alphabet knowledge or fluency) or unconstrained (vocabulary and comprehension; see Figure 1.3). While all of these components are critical to becoming a skilled reader, they develop in distinctly different ways. Constrained, or foundational, skills are limited in scope, develop over a relatively brief period of time, can be taught directly, and can be assessed relatively easily and accurately. The English alphabet is a good example of this: there are only 26 letters; they usually are learned by the end of kindergarten; they can be taught through direct instruction; and it is easy to assess which of the letters a given student knows.

   Unconstrained skills, on the other hand, incorporate an extensive knowledge base, develop over a lifetime, benefit from both direct and indirect instruction, and are difficult to assess fully (Paris, 2005, 2008). Think about vocabulary learning: English words number nearly 250,000; they are learned over a lifetime; while a limited number of words can be taught directly, the majority are learned indirectly; and it is impossible to do more than sample a learner's knowledge. Yet, despite these differences, both constrained and unconstrained skills must be part

Term	Definition	Example
Print concepts	The knowledge of conventions that occur in text	Recognizing that the spaces on either side of a letter or group of letters indicate a distinct word
Phonological awareness	The ability to identify and manipulate units (e.g., words, syllables, phonemes) in oral language	Understanding that *fish* is composed of three separable sounds: f/i/sh
Phonics and word recognition	The identification of words, whether in isolation or in context, in order to determine pronunciation and meaning	Knowing that *s* and *h* in *grasshopper* differs from *sh* in *shop*
Fluency	The combination of accuracy, automaticity, and prosody in reading to facilitate comprehension	Incorporating accurate, automatic word recognition and appropriate pacing to support understanding

FIGURE 1.2. Essential concepts for your foundational skills knowledge.

Category	Examples	Characteristics
Constrained skills	• Print concepts • Phonological awareness • Phonics and word recognition • Fluency	• Limited in scope • Develop over a relatively brief period of time • Can be taught directly • Can be assessed relatively easily and accurately
Unconstrained skills	• Vocabulary • Comprehension	• Extensive knowledge base develops over a lifetime • Benefit from both direct and indirect instruction • Difficult to assess fully

FIGURE 1.3. Constrained versus unconstrained skills.

of effective literacy instruction if learners are to become proficient, engaged readers.

The CCSS authors have made the distinction between constrained and unconstrained skills quite visible. In contrast to the authors of the Report of the National Reading Panel (National Institute of Child Health and Human Development, 2000), who targeted five areas of reading development (phonemic awareness, decoding, fluency, vocabulary, and comprehension) as if they were equally important, the CCSS deals with constrained skills separately from unconstrained ones. The anchor standards in the CCSS are unconstrained (and challenging!); they target deep comprehension of challenging text in multiple genres *and* they give writing and reading equal billing. The constrained skills, on the other hand, are positioned together in the foundational skills section of the Standards and have been somewhat expanded. Figure 1.4 provides a preview.

Given the complexity of reading development (e.g., Chall, 1996; McKenna & Stahl, 2009), it is important not only to think about when various types of instruction should take place, but also why. Since the ultimate goal of reading is the construction of meaning, it is also important to consider how various aspects of literacy instruction contribute to this goal. We briefly discuss several aspects of reading development (print concepts, phonological awareness, decoding/word recognition, vocabulary, and comprehension) before returning to the main focus of this book, fluency and its role in skilled reading.

Print Concepts

Young learners, commonly called emergent readers, need a range of skills to help them succeed as readers (Beauchat, Blamey, & Walpole, 2010; Hayes & Flanigan, 2014; Snow, Burns, & Griffin, 1998). Many of these center around comfort with books (book-handling knowledge) and knowledge of text (e.g., print conventions;

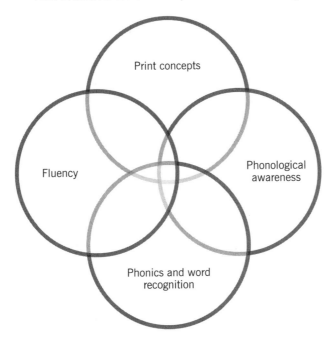

FIGURE 1.4. Targets in foundational skills.

Clay, 2000). When learning about books, students must learn the difference between the front of the book and the back, that in English text runs from left to right and wraps back again to the next line, and that print (not pictures) carry the message of the story.

Additionally, children must develop concept of word, or recognize that spoken words are represented in written language by specific sequences of letters and separated by spaces in print, phonemic awareness, and automatic recognition of upper- and lowercase letters and the sounds associated with them. This knowledge often develops through play with oral and written language as well as modeling by teachers, other literate adults, and older children. Activities can be as varied as reciting nursery rhymes and tongue twisters, creating play centers like restaurants and post offices, or having alphabet or predictable books read to them.

For some children, emergent literacy skills develop in the home, often while sitting on the lap of a parent or other caregiver. For others, this development takes place in a preschool setting or in the kindergarten classroom through the use of Big Books, center time, and an environment rich in print (Edwards, Paratore, & Roser, 2009; Snow et al., 1998). Either way, the skills children need to learn are varied, but their development ultimately helps students navigate text. Further, while emergent literacy skills are still developed through books and other print media such as magazines, increasingly children are transferring (or even initially learning) aspects of what they have learned to electronic text as well (Labbo, 2005;

McKenna, Labbo, Conradi, & Baxter, 2011). Although young students are "digital natives" (Prensky, 2001, p. 1), these skills need to be developed for both forms of texts. Fortunately, many of the concepts about print that students acquire are consistent across a range of media, despite the fact that the pages of digital books turn differently and there are opportunities in electronic texts to explore in a nonlinear manner using links that simply don't exist in traditional print formats (McKenna et al., 2011; Taffe & Bauer, 2013).

Critically, emergent skills must be connected to actual reading—and this reading can and should include both fiction and nonfiction texts (e.g., Hamilton & Schwanenflugel, 2011; Kletzien & Dreher, 2004). By providing learners with a range of genres, including stories, informational text, and poetry, children are exposed to the extensive concepts and vocabulary that are necessary for later school success. Ultimately, this ability to navigate text in its many forms provides the basis for further reading development. According to the CCSS, many of these skills (directionality, concept of word, alphabet knowledge) should be established in kindergarten while the remaining skills (e.g., sentence features such as beginning with an uppercase letter) should be a teaching focus in first grade (see Figure 1.5). And, given their critical importance to early reading success, it is especially important that they be part of the literacy curriculum in these grades.

Phonological Awareness

Another area that is critical to early literacy development is phonological awareness, which begins with the understanding that units in oral language (e.g., individual words) can be identified and manipulated (Beauchat et al., 2010; Hayes & Flanigan, 2014). While this seems obvious to successful readers, it is actually a concept that develops as we become literate. In fact, we hear oral language as a stream of sounds; it is only as we learn about words, syllables, and discrete sounds that we become aware of them. While some students learn about these concepts through language play at home, others will need to learn about them at school.

Kindergarten	Demonstrate understanding of the organization and basic features of print.
	1. Follow words from left to right, top to bottom, and page by page. 2. Recognize that spoken words are represented in written language by specific sequences of letters. 3. Understand that words are separated by spaces in print. 4. Recognize and name all upper- and lowercase letters of the alphabet.
First grade	Demonstrate understanding of the organization and basic features of print.
	1. Recognize the distinguishing features of a sentence (e.g., first word, capitalization, ending punctuation).

FIGURE 1.5. CCSS print concepts by grade level.

Fortunately, they can be developed through a range of "games" that help students recognize these distinct units. These instructional activities involve teaching students to identify words in sentences, syllables in words, onsets and rimes in syllables, and, finally, phonemes, which are the smallest units of sound.

It is also important to be aware that there is not a lockstep developmental approach that requires you to teach phonological awareness prior to teaching the alphabet or beginning decoding instruction. In fact, the two can work hand-in-hand to help your students develop the important early literacy skills that will ensure their reading success from the very beginning of school. For example, by reading alphabet books to your students, you are helping them develop both their knowledge of letters and the sounds associated with them (Bradley & Jones, 2007). Further, while there are still numerous basic alphabet books in which letters and simple objects are the only concepts presented (e.g., *b* is for *ball*), there are others that can expand students' conceptual knowledge as well. For example, *D Is for Drinking Gourd: An African American Alphabet* (Sanders, 2009), *The Folks in the Valley: A Pennsylvania Dutch ABC* (Aylesworth, 1994), *The Ocean Alphabet Book* (Pallotta, 1986), and *Alphabet of Space* (*Smithsonian Alphabet Book*; Galvin, 2006) all have rich vocabulary and present ideas that can expand children's conceptual knowledge (Hirsch, 2003) while developing phonemic awareness and alphabet knowledge.

Since phonological awareness provides a critical foundation upon which children base their reading development, we agree with the CCSS authors who consider kindergarten and first grade to be the ideal time for their instruction. Accordingly, playing with rhyming words, identifying onsets and rimes, and phonemic awareness activities are appropriate for kindergarteners, whereas blending and segmenting phonemes and recognizing long and short vowels are suitable tasks for first graders. However, you should treat these guidelines as recommendations and use your judgment regarding which of your students need this instruction. In other words, if some of your students already have these concepts in place, they are unlikely to benefit from further instruction. On the other hand, you may have some first graders who have not established phonemic awareness; in this case, you may need to focus on more basic concepts. The complete list for the CCSS is provided in Figure 1.6.

Phonics and Word Recognition

Many young readers learn to recognize some highly meaningful (e.g., the child's name) or high-frequency (e.g., *the, and, cat*) words as part of their emergent literacy experiences (Bear, Invernizzi, Templeton, & Johnston, 2011; Ehri, 1995). And some even make the generalizations that allow them to become readers through this informal learning. However, most children learn to recognize the majority of words only after decoding instruction. Decoding instruction incorporates teaching

Kindergarten	Demonstrate understanding of spoken words, syllables, and sounds (phonemes).
	1. Recognize and produce rhyming words.
	2. Count, pronounce, blend, and segment syllables in spoken words.
	3. Blend and segment onsets and rimes of single-syllable spoken words.
	4. Isolate and pronounce the initial, medial vowel, and final sounds (phonemes) in three-phoneme (consonant–vowel–consonant, or CVC) words. (This does not include CVCs ending with /l/, /r/, or /x/.)
	5. Add or substitute individual sounds (phonemes) in simple, one-syllable words to make new words.
First grade	Demonstrate understanding of spoken words, syllables, and sounds (phonemes).
	1. Distinguish long from short vowel sounds in spoken single-syllable words.
	2. Orally produce single-syllable words by blending sounds (phonemes), including consonant blends.
	3. Isolate and pronounce initial, medial vowel, and final sounds (phonemes) in spoken single-syllable words.
	4. Segment spoken single-syllable words into their complete sequence of individual sounds (phonemes).

FIGURE 1.6. CCSS phonological awareness concepts by grade level.

of phonics, high frequency words, and other forms of word study. When such instruction is envisioned broadly (e.g., teaching of root words, derivational endings), it occurs over multiple years (see Figure 1.7 for the list of which phonics and word recognition elements to teach when). And while some aspects of decoding may be beneficial across the grades, decoding should be a central focus for the literacy curriculum of first graders (e.g., Adams, 2011; Chall, 1996). It is also the case that the majority of words that young learners encounter in text are already part of their oral vocabulary; as such, once readers identify a word, they often have access to its meaning.

The ability to decode is critical to becoming a skilled reader, allowing learners to connect written text to spoken language (Adams, 2011). And while certain aspects of decoding instruction can occur in isolation, practice must also occur with connected text if students are to transfer what they learned to actual reading. Stahl (1992) pointed out, in many basal readers or literature anthologies "the patterns taught in the phonics lessons appear infrequently in the text, leading students to believe that phonics is somehow unrelated to the task of reading" (p. 622). One way to ensure that your students understand the critical connection between decoding instruction and reading connected text is to ensure there is a match between the two (Juel & Roper/Schneider, 1985). In other words, it is important that the phonics elements you teach (e.g., short *a*) appear frequently in the texts you and your students are reading (e.g., *Angus and the Cat* [Flack, 1931]; Trachtenburg, 1990). By so doing, you are allowing your students to better consolidate their word recognition skills than they would otherwise (Hiebert, 2010; Logan, 1997; Mostow & Beck, 2005).

Kindergarten	**Know and apply grade-level phonics and word analysis skills in decoding words.**
	1. Demonstrate basic knowledge of one-to-one letter–sound correspondences by producing the primary sound or many of the most frequent sounds for each consonant.
	2. Associate the long and short sounds with common spellings (graphemes) for the five major vowels.
	3. Read common high-frequency words by sight (e.g., *the, of, to, you, she, my, is, are, do, does*).
	4. Distinguish between similarly spelled words by identifying the sounds of the letters that differ.
First grade	**Know and apply grade-level phonics and word analysis skills in decoding words.**
	1. Know the spelling–sound correspondences for common consonant digraphs.
	2. Decode regularly spelled one-syllable words.
	3. Know final -e and common vowel team conventions for representing long vowel sounds.
	4. Use knowledge that every syllable must have a vowel sound to determine the number of syllables in a printed word.
	5. Decode two-syllable words following basic patterns by breaking the words into syllables.
	6. Read words with inflectional endings.
	7. Recognize and read grade-appropriate irregularly spelled words.
Second grade	**Know and apply grade-level phonics and word analysis skills in decoding words.**
	1. Distinguish long and short vowels when reading regularly spelled one-syllable words.
	2. Know spelling–sound correspondences for additional common vowel teams.
	3. Decode regularly spelled two-syllable words with long vowels.
	4. Decode words with common prefixes and suffixes.
	5. Identify words with inconsistent but common spelling–sound correspondences.
	6. Recognize and read grade-appropriate irregularly spelled words.
Third grade	**Know and apply grade-level phonics and word analysis skills in decoding words.**
	1. Identify and know the meaning of the most common prefixes and derivational suffixes.
	2. Decode words with common Latin suffixes.
	3. Decode multisyllable words.
	4. Read grade-appropriate irregularly spelled words.
Fourth grade	**Know and apply grade-level phonics and word analysis skills in decoding words.**
	1. Use combined knowledge of all letter–sound correspondences, syllabication patterns, and morphology (e.g., roots and affixes) to read accurately unfamiliar multisyllabic words in context and out of context.
Fifth grade	**Know and apply grade-level phonics and word analysis skills in decoding words.**
	1. Use combined knowledge of all letter–sound correspondences, syllabication patterns, and morphology (e.g., roots and affixes) to read accurately unfamiliar multisyllabic words in context and out of context.

FIGURE 1.7. CCSS phonics and word recognition concepts by grade level.

Vocabulary and Comprehension

While vocabulary and comprehension are usually dealt with separately, we are discussing them together because we strongly believe that students need "knowledge of words and the world" (Hirsch, 2003, p. 10) to make sense of what they are reading. Critically, the two most effective ways to develop students' knowledge of both new concepts and vocabulary is through reading and discussion (Garcia, Pearson, Taylor, Bauer, & Stahl, 2011; Hamilton & Schwanenflugel, 2011; McKeown, Beck, & Blake, 2009). In practical terms, this reinforces the importance of exposing your students to a wide range of reading material (Adams, 2010–2011; Cunningham & Stanovich, 1998) involving both a broad selection of genres and topics as well as a range of difficulty levels or degree of challenge (e.g., Halladay, 2012; Hiebert, 2002; Reutzel, Jones, Fawson, & Smith, 2008).

One way to assist students with challenging texts is by reading across a theme. This increases the likelihood that students will encounter vocabulary and concepts in multiple contexts—both deepening and broadening their knowledge base. We have created several lists of books organized by theme to get you started. These lists can be found on pp. 97–100. Given the importance of high-quality challenging children's literature across the curriculum, we have also included several lists of award-winning and notable books on pp. 101–136. These selections include science and social studies books as well as fiction. Some of the awards are very familiar (e.g., the Newbery and Caldecott awards) and some less so (e.g., the Carter G. Woodson Award and the Sibert Medal). While not all of the lists are designed exclusively for primary grade students, there are appropriate selections for young readers on each of the lists.

There are multiple ways to integrate effective vocabulary and comprehension instruction into the classroom (Silverman & Meyer, 2014; Stahl & Garcia, in press); however, there are certain general approaches that we recommend as the basis of an effective and meaningful literacy curriculum. To begin with, exposure to complex text with rich vocabulary and conceptual knowledge is critical across all grades (Biemiller, 2003; Hamilton & Schwanenflugel, 2011; Kletzien & Dreher, 2004). For the youngest learners, this means teachers must read aloud from texts as varied as the fictional selections *Stellaluna* (Cannon, 2008) and *Aunt Flossie's Hats (and Crab Cakes Later)* (Howard, 1995) to the nonfiction—and potentially companion—texts *Bats!* (Carney, 2010) and *Goliath: Hero of the Great Baltimore Fire* (Friddell, 2010).

As students become increasingly capable of reading themselves, this broad exposure to reading material can occur through a variety of strategies that involve their own reading. These can be as simple as integrating partner reading (see Chapter 4), shared reading (Stahl, 2012), or scaffolded silent reading (Reutzel et al., 2008) into the reading curriculum or can be somewhat more involved, incorporating approaches such as reciprocal teaching (Palincsar & Brown, 1986) or the directed reading–thinking activity (DRTA; Stauffer, 1971). Ultimately, it is this exposure to a range of concepts and vocabulary that allows students to begin to close the achievement gap and provides them with the understandings necessary to succeed within the Common Core (e.g., Hirsch & Pondiscio, 2010–2011). See Figure 1.8 for the CCSS recommendations.

Where Does Fluency Fit in Reading Development?

When thinking about the role various components play in reading development, it is important to consider where fluency fits into the overall process. We see fluency as a link between word recognition and comprehension, allowing learners to shift their focus from print to meaning (Kuhn, Schwanenflugel, & Meisinger, 2010). This occurs because fluency enables learners' word recognition to move from laborious to automatic. It also allows learners to apply elements of oral language to written text; these aspects of fluency, collectively known as prosody, include the use of correct intonation and appropriate phrasing. Prosodic reading also contributes to learners' comprehension of text by helping them recognize shades of meaning that otherwise might be unrecognizable. It is this combination of accurate, automatic word recognition and prosodic phrasing that make fluency a central component in reading development and in students' construction of meaning from text.

Ultimately, the following definition best expresses our understanding of fluent reading: "Fluency combines accuracy, automaticity, and oral reading prosody, which, taken together, facilitate the reader's construction of meaning. It is

LITERATURE	
Stories	Includes children's adventure stories, folktales, legends, fables, fantasy, realistic fiction, and myth.
Dramas	Includes staged dialogue and brief familiar scenes.
Poetry	Includes nursery rhymes and the subgenres of the narrative poem, limerick, and free verse poem.
INFORMATIONAL TEXT	
Literary nonfiction and historical, scientific, and technical texts	Includes biographies and autobiographies; books about history, social studies, science, and the arts; technical texts, including directions, forms, and information displayed in graphs, charts, or maps; and digital sources on a range of topics.

FIGURE 1.8. Range of text types for CCSS. Standard 10: range, quality, and complexity of student reading, grades K–5.

demonstrated during oral reading through ease of word recognition, appropriate pacing, phrasing, and intonation. It is a factor in both oral and silent reading that can limit or support comprehension" (Kuhn et al., 2010, p. 242). While the rest of this book will be dedicated to discussing reading fluency in detail, we want you to bear this definition in mind when considering how best to support fluency through instruction. Finally, we believe that the following chapters will help you implement instruction that makes this definition a reality in your classrooms.

CHAPTER 2
. . . .

What Is Fluent Reading?

GUIDING QUESTIONS
....

- What are the components of reading fluency?
- How does automaticity contribute to comprehension?
- How does prosody contribute to comprehension?
- How does fluent reading differ between kindergarten, first, second, and third grades, and beyond?
- In what ways is fluency important for the CCSS?

As we mentioned in Chapter 1, our definition of fluency includes three critical components: accuracy, automaticity, and prosody (Kuhn et al., 2010; see Figure 2.1). While you may be more familiar with the first two components, all of them make distinct contributions to both fluency and comprehension of text. Our goal for this chapter is to explore the role of automaticity and prosody in this relationship. We will also provide an overview of effective fluency instruction and discuss how such instruction can contribute to student success with the CCSS. Most importantly, we will show you that understanding fluency deeply will help you to address it more quickly and directly. We will start with some technical descriptions of fluency and then move on to its instructional implications.

What Is Fluent Reading?: The Role of Automaticity and Prosody
. . . .

As a skilled reader, when you read out loud, your reading is generally smooth, effortless, and expressive (Kuhn et al., 2010). You are able to recognize the vast majority of words you encounter accurately and automatically and are able to

13

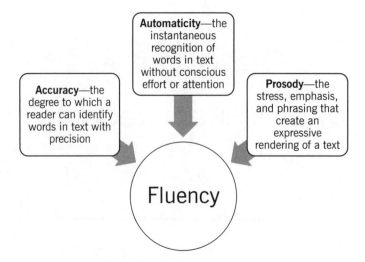

FIGURE 2.1. Components of fluency.

determine appropriate phrasing and intonation. In other words, your reading is fluent. Being fluent not only ensures automaticity and expression, it contributes to comprehension. We focus on fluency not for its own sake, but because it helps children construct meaning from text. So how does fluency contribute to comprehension? The answer involves both automaticity and prosody, and our discussion of these components should lead to a fuller understanding of fluency than can develop from a focus on automaticity alone (Applegate et al., 2009; Kuhn et al., 2010; see Figure 2.2). Before we begin this discussion, however, we need to mention that while a base of accurate word recognition must be established before students can become fluent readers, we will not cover decoding instruction in this book (see Hayes & Flanigan, 2014, for effective phonics and word recognition instruction). Instead, we will concentrate on a range of best practices that allows students' word recognition to become automatic and their reading to incorporate appropriate intonation.

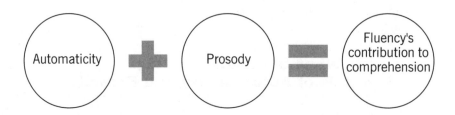

FIGURE 2.2. The relationship between fluency and comprehension.

The Role of Automaticity

If students are to make sense of what they read, they need to accurately and automatically identify written words (e.g., Chall, 1996; National Institute of Child Health and Human Development, 2000). Initially, this involves students becoming comfortable at recognizing words that can be easily decoded and high-frequency (sometimes phonetically irregular) words. However, when students are first learning to read, this process often requires them to focus on each word they encounter, resulting in reading that sounds stilted and uneven. In fact, it is often the case that students at this stage of development spend so much time figuring out every word in a sentence, they are unable to focus on the meaning of the sentence as a whole. Instruction in word recognition, in a variety of formats (e.g., Bear et al., 2011; Hayes & Flanigan, 2014; Trachtenburg, 1990), will help students build their sight vocabulary and make the generalizations needed to become skilled readers. However, decoding instruction is necessary but insufficient to ensure that students become fluent.

The inability of students to focus on meaning while learning how to decode can best be explained through automaticity theory (e.g., LaBerge & Samuels, 1974; Logan, 1997; see Figure 2.3). This theory posits that we have a limited amount of attention available for any complex task. As a result, when we encounter new activities that incorporate multiple components, it is difficult for us to concentrate on all aspects simultaneously. Think about individuals first learning to play a sport or a musical instrument. Novices need to learn the various steps in order to be successful, whether this means learning to dribble or practicing scales. At the

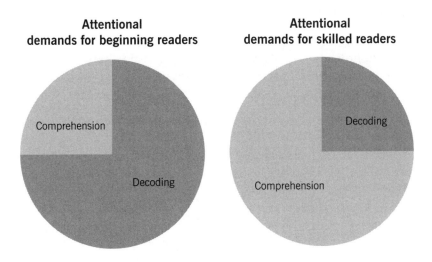

FIGURE 2.3. The division of attention between decoding and comprehension for beginning and skilled readers.

same time, if we are to move past the basics, certain aspects of these tasks need to become effortless or automatic. In the case of reading, since comprehension should always receive the bulk of our attention, it is our decoding that needs to become automatic.

For teachers, one of the most important questions at this stage of development is, "How does decoding become automatic?" The answer is simple. Practice. This means ensuring that students have extensive opportunities to figure out words both in guided instruction and independent practice (e.g., Bear et al., 2011). Such opportunities allow them to develop comfort with the spelling patterns, or orthography, that comprise written English.

However, while word study of all types is an essential component of the literacy curriculum, if students are to become fluent readers, it is also critical that they have plenty of opportunities to apply their developing knowledge to reading (Kuhn, 2004–2005; Reutzel et al., 2008). This reading can involve books, magazines, poetry, or material from the Internet. Without this additional step, however, students are likely to become very good at recognizing words in isolation, but not nearly as likely to become fluent readers. In other words, it will be difficult for them to transfer what they are learning to connected text—in the same way that those who are adept at playing scales will never become great musicians unless they practice playing actual songs. On the other hand, when you provide students with abundant opportunities to read a wide selection of material—with appropriate support where necessary—the likelihood that they will develop automaticity increases significantly.

The Role of Prosody

While automaticity provides insight into certain aspects of fluency's relationship to comprehension, prosody also plays a critical role. Prosody itself consists of several elements: intonation, stress, pacing, and the rhythmic patterns of language (e.g., Benjamin & Schwanenflugel, 2010; Erekson, 2003; see Figure 2.4). When reading,

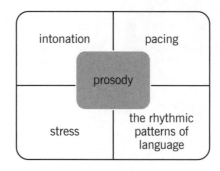

FIGURE 2.4. The components of prosody.

these elements work together to provide shades of meaning and help us determine appropriate expression and phrasing. To some degree, prosodic elements are represented by punctuation like commas, periods, semicolons, and the use of italics. This can be seen in the title joke of Lynn Truss's (2003) *Eats, Shoots and Leaves*:

> A panda walks into a café. He orders a sandwich, eats it, then draws a gun and fires two shots into the air.
>
> "Why?" asks the confused waiter, as the panda makes towards the exit. The panda produces a badly punctuated wildlife manual and tosses it over his shoulder.
>
> "I'm a panda," he says, at the door. "Look it up."
>
> The waiter turns to the relevant entry and, sure enough, finds an explanation.
>
> "**Panda.** Large black-and-white bear-like mammal, native to China. Eats, shoots and leaves." (back cover)

Unfortunately, many aspects of prosody that exist in speech cannot be represented by punctuation. For example, it is usually clear where phrasing exists in spoken language, but this is less apparent in writing (e.g., Miller & Schwanenflugel, 2006); and while some phrases are identified through commas, others are not. Look at this sentence from Faulkner's *Absalom, Absalom!*:

> From a little after two o'clock until almost sundown of the long still hot weary dead September afternoon they sat in what Miss Coldfield still called the office because her father had called it that—a dim hot airless room with the blinds all closed and fastened for forty-three summers because when she was a girl someone had believed that light and moving air carried heat and that dark was always cooler, and which (as the sun shone fuller and fuller on that side of the house) became latticed with yellow slashes full of dust motes which Quentin thought of as being flecks of the dead old dried paint itself blown inward from the scaling blinds as wind might have blown them. (2012, p. 3)

Another writer might have used a comma after the words *September afternoon* to indicate a dependent clause and assist the reader in identifying a phrasal boundary. In Faulkner's case, it is left to the reader to determine where the grouping of words, or parsing, needs to occur. While skilled readers may initially read through this passage with few breaks, they are likely to reread in order to construct a more nuanced sense of the author's intended meaning.

Although young readers are not going to encounter text of this complexity, the fact that they often read word-by-word or in two- or three-word phrases creates comparable difficulties in their attempts to determine meaning in the selections they *are* reading. Importantly, a series of studies (e.g., Casteel, 1988; Cromer, 1970; Weiss, 1983) demonstrated that disfluent readers across a range of ages actually improved their comprehension when the text was organized into appropriate phrase units for them.

Similar problems occur with expression (e.g., Benjamin & Schwanenflugel, 2010). It is often the case that the location of the stress or intonation affects the meaning of the words or sentences; so, for example, if you were driving in the country, got a flat tire, and responded by saying, "That's just great," it would be clear to a listener that you were not happy. However, when reading this sentence, that sense of irony is not visible in the words on the page. Instead, you need to understand the situation in order to understand how to interpret the comment. Again, this is something skilled readers are able to do fairly readily. Unfortunately, given the multiple tasks young learners need to coordinate as they read, such nuances may be lost on them, causing them to draw incorrect conclusions.

While the above examples illustrate our point, you can imagine how readers' inability to apply aspects of oral language to text can contribute to misunderstandings. On the plus side, not only are these skills that learners can develop through their own reading, they can also be taught. And, helping children to become prosodic readers also helps them develop better comprehension as well (Kuhn et al., 2010). Therefore, when considering fluency's overall contribution to comprehension, we feel it is important not only to ensure that your students are reading relatively accurately and at a reasonable pace, but also with the expressiveness that replicates oral language.

What Does Effective Fluency Instruction Look Like?

An understanding of fluency that includes prosody as well as automaticity has important implications for instruction. Rather than simply teaching your students to read as quickly as possible, a process that can actually distract from the construction of meaning, it is important to teach them to read with appropriate pacing and expression (e.g., Kuhn et al., 2010; Samuels, 2007). In fact, there are several principles that underlie effective fluency instruction (Rasinski, 1989, 2004a); these are: modeling, providing extensive opportunities for practice, ensuring sufficient support or scaffolding, and incorporating prosodic elements in your instruction (see Figure 2.5).

It is hard to tease out these four principles completely because they are very much intertwined, but we will begin with modeling. In this case, modeling occurs by demonstrating good fluent reading—so that students know what their goal is. This is especially important as they make the transition from stilted beginning reading to reading that is smooth and expressive. Your oral reading provides them with a sense of what their reading should (and will!) sound like. Modeling can also help create a sense of community within your classroom and instill a love of reading among your students.

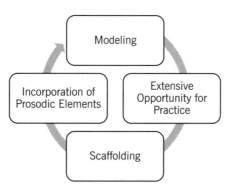

FIGURE 2.5. Principles of effective fluency instruction.

Further, there is a variety of material that is best presented orally. Think about the joys of listening to poems, plays, highly descriptive narratives, and gripping pieces of nonfiction read aloud (e.g., Rasinski, 1989). Using such a broad selection of reading material is especially important for two reasons (e.g., Kletzien & Dreher, 2004). First, since not all learners are enamored by fiction, reading from a broad variety of texts increases the likelihood that you will validate the interests of all your learners, not just some of them. Second, by introducing your students to genres that they might not otherwise encounter, you may kindle an interest in an entirely new category of reading. We know of one student who only wanted to read fantasies, but ended up enjoying biographies and history once his teacher read several of them to the class. Ultimately, you may find that reading aloud serves as a motivator for your students' independent reading and broadens their knowledge and interests.

Despite the positives of modeling fluent reading through read-alouds, there are certain cautions we feel are worth considering (e.g., Kuhn & Schwanenflugel, 2007). If students are to become fluent readers, they need to spend the majority of their literacy period developing their own reading skills, not listening to their teacher read. So while reading to your learners can be enjoyable and motivating, it should not last for a significant period of time. Five to ten minutes of teacher read-aloud time during reading instruction seems to be reasonable, although you may extend that time if you use a read-aloud as a part of your shared reading period or during your social studies and science instruction. However, careful use of your time is especially important when dealing with challenging material. And while reading aloud to your learners or the use of some form of round-robin reading may seem to be an effective way of providing them with access to such texts, it is far better that you provide them with enough scaffolding to read the text themselves. We will provide you with effective approaches to such student reading in Chapter 4.

Modeling, like word recognition, is necessary but not sufficient to ensure fluent reading. Instead, you need to both provide your learners with extensive

NOT ALL FLUENCY PRACTICE IS EQUAL
(OR THE *DON'TS* OF FLUENCY INSTRUCTION)

Unfortunately, not all "fluency practice" makes for effective instruction. Below we present several practices that we strongly believe should be kept out of your literacy curriculum. After reading through them, we hope you will agree.

1. *Don't focus on speed or word recognition in isolation.* If students are to become fluent readers, they must develop automaticity. However, developing automatic word recognition—in text or in isolation—does not necessarily lead to fluent reading. Rather than focusing simply on reading quickly, effective fluency instruction must involve reading connected text in ways that emphasize not only accurate and automatic word recognition but also the appropriate use of expression and phrasing.

2. *Don't rely on short passages or repeated readings.* Unfortunately, when using repeated readings with short texts, students may develop the notion that good reading is fast reading. Further, brief passages and short poems do not provide readers with nearly enough time actually reading connected text to develop their fluency. As we emphasize throughout this book, if students are to become skilled readers, they need to spend substantial amounts of time reading texts that are both challenging and of sufficient length.

3. *Don't overuse Readers' Theatre.* We have witnessed "Readers' Theatre" being used as a surrogate for round-robin reading; in these cases, each student was assigned a small section of text that she or he was required to read aloud. As a result, they only had the opportunity to read a few lines each. To make matters worse, much of the period was spent determining which reader should read which part. If you use this approach, we suggest that you use it sparingly, make sure everyone has the opportunity to read a substantial amount of text, and assign the parts quickly so students can spend most of their class time actually reading.

4. *Don't use easy texts for instruction.* We have seen students who are accurate but slow readers reassigned to easier texts in the hope that their reading rate would improve. If your students are reading such selections with high levels of comprehension, your goal should be developing their automaticity with these texts rather than providing them with easier material. Such a focus should allow them to increase their reading rate while continuing to work with the type of challenging texts they are capable of comprehending.

5. *Don't forget that the ultimate goal of reading is comprehension.* Finally, while fluency is important, how quickly the students read or how well they sound when reading aloud is only useful in the service of understanding the text they are reading. If you emphasize the construction of meaning in all your lessons, your students will learn not only to be fluent readers, but readers who comprehend as well.

opportunities to practice reading themselves and ensure that you give them enough support, or scaffolding, to experience success. Such practice allows students to consolidate what they are learning. We know that for a large number of students the opportunity to read is still limited (Hiebert & Martin, 2009; Kuhn & Schwanenflugel, 2007). Ultimately, unless students are provided with such opportunities, they are far less likely to develop the ability to read fluently.

It is also the case that, when readers encounter challenging material (selections at the top end of their instructional level or the beginning of their frustration level), the provision of scaffolding can allow them access to the text. This is especially true for texts that contain new vocabulary or concepts. It is also the case that the more difficult a text is, the greater the amount of support that is required. Nor are reading levels stagnant. A child who is interested in space exploration will likely be able to read more challenging material on that topic than, say, on colonial history. And while *Junie B. Jones and the Stupid Smelly Bus* (Park, 1992) and *A Chair for My Mother* (Williams, 2007) may be labeled at the same level of difficulty, the latter is more conceptually challenging than the former.

The final instructional principle for building fluency involves incorporating prosody (Kuhn et al., 2010; Rasinski, 1989). As we mentioned earlier in the chapter, when children fail to use prosodic elements, comprehension can suffer. By teaching students to apply appropriate phrasing and expression, through modeling, explanation, and direct instruction, you are linking the characteristics of oral and written language. We believe it is particularly important to highlight this principle given the emphasis on reading rate that has occurred in recent years. To a large extent, this focus has arisen in response to a misuse of screening measures designed to measure rate without correspondingly measuring prosody. Unfortunately, this practice can have negative consequences, causing learners to focus on rate at the expense of their understanding.

Rather than attempting to increase your students' reading rate per se, we would argue that a more effective approach involves a focus on improving their pacing. In other words, you should encourage your children to read at a reasonable rate with appropriate phrasing and expression and emphasize the goal of comprehension. Not only does this better match our understanding of what it means to be a fluent reader, it also matches our broader goal of creating skilled, engaged readers who are able to deal successfully with a wide range of texts. Luckily, these principles are integrated into the fluency routines that we will present to you throughout this book.

Where Is Fluency in the CCSS?

Fluency is an essential component of the CCSS. First, fluent reading is a distinct goal for the elementary grades (Common Core State Standards Initiative, 2012);

we presented the fluency standards by grade level in Chapter 1. Second, fluency underlies the broader skills that are critical to success with these standards, what E. D. Hirsch (2003) calls "knowledge of words and the world." While we agree with the CCSS's highlighting of fluency goals by grade level, we feel it is important to think about these standards in a slightly more nuanced way; this understanding connects to the developmental view we presented in Chapter 1.

The CCSS for Fluency

For kindergarteners, the CCSS state that students should "read emergent-reader texts with purpose and understanding" (see Figure 2.6). Since learners at this stage are usually pretend reading, it is important that you afford them opportunities both

Kindergarteners	Grade 1 Students	Grade 2 Students
Read emergent-reader texts with purpose and understanding	Read with sufficient accuracy and fluency to support comprehension. 1. Read on-level text with purpose and understanding. 2. Read on-level text orally with accuracy, appropriate rate, and expression on successive readings. 3. Use context to confirm or self-correct word recognition and understanding, rereading as necessary.	Read with sufficient accuracy and fluency to support comprehension. 1. Read on-level text with purpose and understanding. 2. Read on-level text orally with accuracy, appropriate rate, and expression on successive readings. 3. Use context to confirm or self-correct word recognition and understanding, rereading as necessary.
Grade 3 Students	**Grade 4 Students**	**Grade 5 Students**
Read with sufficient accuracy and fluency to support comprehension. 1. Read on-level text with purpose and understanding. 2. Read on-level prose and poetry orally with accuracy, appropriate rate, and expression on successive readings. 3. Use context to confirm or self-correct word recognition and understanding, rereading as necessary.	Read with sufficient accuracy and fluency to support comprehension. 1. Read on-level text with purpose and understanding. 2. Read on-level prose and poetry orally with accuracy, appropriate rate, and expression on successive readings. 3. Use context to confirm or self-correct word recognition and understanding, rereading as necessary.	Read with sufficient accuracy and fluency to support comprehension. 1. Read on-level text with purpose and understanding. 2. Read on-level prose and poetry orally with accuracy, appropriate rate, and expression on successive readings. 3. Use context to confirm or self-correct word recognition and understanding, rereading as necessary.

FIGURE 2.6. CCSS reading standards: Foundational skills, K–5. From Common Core State Standards Initiative (2012, pp. 16–17). Copyright by the National Governors Association Center for Best Practices and the Council of Chief State School Officers. All rights reserved.

to listen to and to read or reread books and other material themselves (e.g., Hamilton & Schwanenflugel, 2011). This can occur during centers, through whole-class shared readings (including the reading of science or social studies texts aloud), and through small-group activities. Giving your students a range of experiences allows them to develop the sense of what fluent reading sounds like and will help their pretend reading transition into conventional reading. They will also develop emergent literacy skills in a cohesive way, further laying the foundation for successful reading development.

The standards for the remaining elementary grades state that learners are to "read with sufficient accuracy and fluency to support comprehension" (see Figure 2.6). This involves reading grade-level text "with purpose and understanding," with "accuracy, appropriate rate, and expression on successive readings," and using "context to confirm or self-correct word recognition and understanding, rereading as necessary." These standards provide a clear overview of our goals for fluent reading. And while we have written this volume with primary-grade students and their teachers in mind, the conformity of the CCSS's standards across the grades indicate that the same understandings can be used to incorporate fluency practices in grades 3–5.

At the same time, we are mindful of the developmental nature of reading; as such, it is important to identify what is uniquely appropriate for first and second graders (e.g., Adams, 2011; Chall, 1996). Generally, we expect first graders to enter school with solid emergent literacy skills, including book-handling knowledge, alphabet knowledge, and a small number of words they can recognize automatically (i.e., certain high-frequency, phonetically regular words, such as *the* or *cat*, or highly meaningful words, like their own names). By the end of the year, we expect them to have developed a much higher level of accuracy in terms of word recognition as they take responsibility for reading a greater number of texts. As with any good literacy curriculum, there should always be a focus on comprehension, vocabulary, writing, and oral language development over the course of the year as well. However, developing accurate word recognition is a distinct focus for this age group, allowing them to make the transition from predictable books to a broader range of texts successfully.

The change in focus for word recognition can also be seen in the CWPM (correct words per minute) norms presented for first grade (Hasbrouck & Tindal, 2006; see Table 2.1). These norms were generated from the oral reading samples of first through eighth graders from across the country. You can see that the measurement of reading rate does not even begin until midyear in first grade. This is an indicator that first grade is a transition period in which instruction must build accuracy; the focus only shifts to automaticity toward the second half of the year. In other words, your emphasis should be on consolidating your students' knowledge of sound–symbol correspondences and expanding their recognition of high-frequency words, and assisting them in applying these understandings to connected text.

TABLE 2.1. CWPM Ratings at the 50th Percentile for First, Second, and Third Graders at Three Time Points during the School Year (Fall, Winter, Spring)

	Fall CWPM	Winter CWPM	Spring CWPM
First grade/50th percentile		23	53
Second grade/50th percentile	51	72	89
Third grade/50th percentile	71	92	107

As we mentioned in Chapter 1, you may find your first graders' reading to be choppy and stilted since they are still trying to figure out many of the words; and they are also likely to have difficulty constructing meaning as a result (e.g., Chall, 1996). As your learners continue to develop their word recognition skills over the course of the year, you may want to integrate more of the strategies discussed in the chapters that follow. However, while you will notice that even though your learners are becoming increasingly fluent (their reading rate increases; they shift from word-by-word reading to more frequent use of two- or three-word phrases), first grade is still a time when word work remains the primary focus for foundational skills for most learners.

As you focus on decoding, however, there are several instructional strategies that allow you to integrate effective fluency-oriented instruction into the first-grade literacy curriculum (Dougherty Johnson & Kuhn, 2013). One approach involves having your students reread a passage. This procedure differs from traditional repeated readings insofar as the focus is not increasing reading rate per se; instead, the goals are to help students confirm their decoding and improve their comprehension. As was mentioned in the first chapter, another effective approach involves the use of reading material that reinforces the phonics elements being taught (Stahl, 1992; Trachtenburg, 1990). For example, if you are focusing on the long *o* sound, you could first highlight it through a particular text (*The Giant's Toe* [Cole, 1986] or *The Snowy Day* [Keats, 1976]), then have students work with the concept, and finish by reading an additional text to illustrate the contextualized concept again (e.g., *Why Is It Snowing?* [Williams, 2005] or *Maps and Globes* [Knowlton, 1985]). It is also important that you continue modeling for them by reading aloud from a wide variety of material.

In general, grade two, and to a lesser degree grade three, are the years in which learners traditionally become fluent readers (Chall, 1996; Kuhn & Stahl, 2003). This means that, while some decoding instruction should still occur, your focus should be on developing automaticity and integrating prosodic elements into most of your students' oral reading. The strategies discussed throughout the remainder of this book provide a range of examples for effective instruction. It is at this point, rather than in first grade, that we believe the CCSS expectations for fluency begin to stand on their own in terms of learners' literacy development. And, while the fluency standards remain the same over the remaining elementary grades, your focus on fluency per se should be lessened as students develop as independent readers.

Before leaving this section, we want to emphasize that our presentation of students' literacy development in terms of grades is meant to provide you with a general sense of your learners' growth (e.g., Chall, 1996; McKenna & Stahl, 2009). It is not meant as a lock-step approach. Children are individuals. Their learning will develop at different rates, and it is important for you to adjust your instruction accordingly. Just as you would not spend time teaching phonemic awareness to a student who can already decode, if some of your students are already reading a selection fluently, they can focus on reading material that is different from that of their peers. Similarly, students who are having difficulty making the transition to fluency may benefit from repeated readings even if it is not a necessary instructional approach for most of the class.

Fluent Reading and Challenging Texts

There is one other way in which fluency is important to the CCSS, and we feel it is critical to your learners' success. One of the key principles of the CCSS is the use of challenging text (Common Core State Standards Initiative, 2012). According to the Standards, there is a

> need for college and career ready students to be proficient in reading complex informational text independently in a variety of content areas. Most of the required reading in college and workforce training programs is informational in structure and challenging in content; postsecondary education programs typically provide students with both a higher volume of such reading than is generally required in K–12 schools and comparatively little scaffolding. (p. 4)

Several of the fluency-oriented instructional approaches presented in the remaining chapters of this book lend themselves to the use of such material. And it is also the case that the development of fluency, in its broadest sense, can create the kind of positive reading cycle that allows students to broaden their vocabulary and conceptual knowledge and can lay the basis for further reading success and increased reading stamina (Stanovich, 1986; see Figure 2.7).

Here is a recap. In order to become fluent readers, students will need to read from texts that provide some level of challenge as well as text at their instructional and independent levels (Kuhn & Stahl, 2003). The degree of challenge and the amount of support required are going to vary from situation to situation and

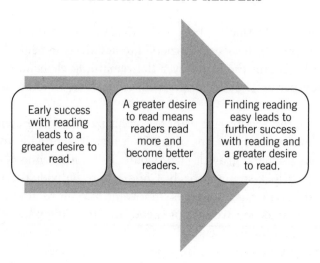

FIGURE 2.7. The positive development experienced by successful readers.

according to the skill level and background knowledge of your learners (Adams, 2010–2011; Cunningham & Stanovich, 1998; see Figure 2.8). As a result, it is important that you remain flexible, varying the amount of support you provide accordingly. The strategies presented throughout the book will help you find the appropriate amount of scaffolding for a given selection. And as tempting as it may be to turn to something easier when students are encountering particularly difficult material, it is critical to remember you must engage and support them, facing the challenge directly, if they are going to be able to tackle such texts independently.

Finally, remember that motivation is also a major factor in students' willingness to read (e.g., Gambrell, 2011). This can best be illustrated by the "playground buzz" that often accompanies a book or series of books that are popular among young readers. When a book takes off in terms of popularity (think about the Goosebumps, Lemony Snickett, and Harry Potter series), even your most

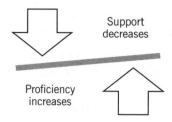

FIGURE 2.8. The amount of support you need to provide decreases as your readers' proficiency increases.

reading-averse students will likely attempt to read them since so many of their friends are clearly enjoying them. It is important to support these attempts, and we will discuss effective ways to do so in the following chapters. On the other hand, you may be able to develop your students' interest in a topic simply through your instruction. If you show enthusiasm, your enjoyment can be contagious—and students will be more likely to engage with texts as a result.

Conclusion

Ultimately, appropriate fluency instruction will be reflected in student success with the type of challenging texts required by the CCSS. Cunningham and Stanovich (1998) put it best for us:

> We should provide all children, regardless of their achievement levels, with as many reading experiences as possible. Indeed, this becomes doubly imperative for precisely those children whose verbal abilities are most in need of bolstering, for it is the very act of reading that can build those capacities. An encouraging message for teachers of low-achieving students is implicit here. We often despair of changing our students' abilities, but there is at least one partially malleable habit that will itself develop abilities—reading! (pp. 7–8)

Let's work together through the rest of this book to make this a reality.

CHAPTER 3
∙ ∙ ∙ ∙ ∙ ∙ ∙ ∙ ∙ ∙ ∙
Assessing Fluent Reading

GUIDING QUESTIONS

- Why is it important to assess fluency?
- What are the components that need to be assessed?
- How can accuracy and automaticity be assessed?
- Why is assessing these two components insufficient?
- How can prosody be assessed?
- How does this contribute to a fuller understanding of fluent reading?

As with most classroom-based assessments, two primary reasons dictate why you might use a fluency assessment with your students. It allows you to track the growth of your students over time (progress monitoring), and it can assist you in identifying which of your students might benefit from fluency instruction (screening). Using the comprehensive definition we provided in Chapter 2, we will look at fluency assessment broadly and provide tools and strategies to evaluate all of its elements.

Why Assess Fluency?

Fluency assessment can be an important part of creating a literacy profile for your students. By listening to their oral reading, you can measure their reading rate and get a sense of their prosody. You can also see how their reading is progressing across a range of material, from classroom texts to standardized screenings (e.g.,

DIBELS [Good & Kaminski, 2002]; AIMSweb [Shinn & Shinn, 2002]) and more comprehensive informal assessments (e.g., Qualitative Reading Inventory–5 [Leslie & Caldwell, 2010]; Basic Reading Inventory [Johns, 2012]). Further, assessment can help you determine how much support your students may need for various selections. For example, you may find that most of your students are at their instructional level (a level at which they are successful with some support) for the material you are using in your grade-level English language arts instruction; on the other hand, these same students may benefit from greater amounts of scaffolding when reading their content-area texts, since these are often more conceptually challenging (see Figure 3.1).

You will also likely have some students who find grade-level material too difficult, even with your assistance. These children may benefit from alternative selections as a way of introducing the subject matter. Or you may have some learners who already have an extensive grasp of material at their grade level and should be given the opportunity to work independently on extension activities or with more challenging selections. Finally, given the continuing importance of reading rate, or correct words per minute (CWPM), in terms of progress monitoring, it is important that you track your students' growth, both individually and as a class. Overall, fluency assessments can help you decide how to implement fluency-oriented instruction in your classroom and provide some guidance regarding text selection as well.

Assessing Accurate and Automatic Word Recognition

Given that fluent reading consists of three central components, it is essential that we address each of them (see Figure 3.2). Since accuracy and automaticity are the most frequently measured components (e.g., Samuels, 2007), we will start with them. Measures of CWPM provide you with a score that combines *accuracy*, or the number of words a reader is able to correctly identify in a text, and *automaticity*, or the rate at which a learner reads a given text, into a single measure. It is also

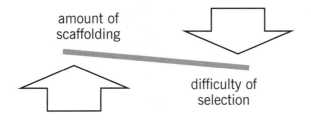

amount of
scaffolding

difficulty of
selection

FIGURE 3.1. The variation in scaffolding based upon the difficulty of a selection.

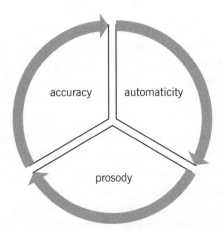

FIGURE 3.2. The components of fluent reading.

the easiest and most concrete way of evaluating fluency. It is this combination of qualities that has made CWPM the most commonly used fluency measure.

Here's how you generate a CWPM score. The basic format involves listening to a student reading aloud from a previously unread text, often called a "cold reading," for 1 minute. It is important to choose a new selection since even a small amount of practice may affect how well the material is read. While the student is reading you should note all *miscues* (any deviation from the text; Clay, 2006; Lesley & Caldwell, 2010; McKenna & Stahl, 2009). In order to do this easily and

---

DETERMINING A CWPM SCORE
WHEN COUNTING ALL MISCUES

1. Identify a previously unread text.
2. Make two copies, one for you and one for the student.
3. Get a watch with a second hand or a stopwatch to record the time and a clipboard and pencil.
4. Count and record the number of words in the passage.
5. Have your student read aloud from the beginning of the passage for 1 minute, marking the last word read.
6. Record any miscues (e.g., insertions, omissions, or substitutions) on your copy.
7. Note any repetitions or particularly quick reading to provide insight into particularly slow or fast reading rates.
8. Count both the total number of words read and the number of miscues; subtract the miscues from total words read to determine the CWPM.

accurately, it is important for you to have a copy of the selection to write on. Make sure you also have either a watch with a second hand or a stopwatch along with a clipboard and pencil.

Next, determine the number of words in a given passage to help make your computation easier. Have your student start reading from the beginning of the passage and ask him or her to stop at the 1-minute mark. Listen carefully and record any miscues the student makes on your copy of the text; mark the last word the student reads. When counting miscues, we include omissions (students skipping a word), substitutions (student replacing one word with a different one, even when the substituted word has a similar spelling, a similar meaning, or both), or insertions (students adding a word that is not written in the text). You may also want to note any repetitions; while repetitions do not count as errors, they can help to explain a slower reading rate. Similarly, if your student is rushing through the material, you will want to note this fact since it may help explain a faster reading rate. At this point, you should count up the total number of words the student has read, determine the number of miscues, and simply subtract the number of miscues from the number of words read for your CWPM total.

Before moving on to an example, it is important that we note a second way of scoring a student's CWPM rating. If you are using a curriculum-based measure (CBM), insertions are not counted as miscues (Fuchs & Fuchs, 2007). This is because any insertion results in a slower overall reading time; as such, counting them could be viewed as a double penalty for the reader. However, whether you choose to count insertions as miscues will likely depend both on whether your school is using CBMs and on the degree of analysis you will be undertaking with your students' reading. We show just such an analysis with the example of one first-grade student, Eric, and present both versions of the miscue totals for the demonstrated passage so you can compare them.

Let's look at Eric's oral reading and CWPM rating. Eric was evaluated at the end of the school year along with the rest of his class. His teacher asked him to read from *Little Bear* by Elsa Holmelund Minarik (1978), a text that is considered to be at the late first-grade-reading level. He reached the 64th word in a 77-word passage in 1 minute. He had one insertion (*out*), three omissions (*something*; *your head*), and eight substitutions, for a total CWPM rating of 52. According to the oral reading fluency norms presented by Timothy Rasinski (2004b; see Table 3.1), this places Eric in the target range for his grade and time of year—he is reading 52 CWPM. However, many of Eric's miscues result from his overreliance on the illustrations; over the course of the three pages, Little Bear is looking out the window at the snow, getting ready to go out, and putting on a hat to keep warm. Each of these pictures pair up with certain of his miscues (e.g., "It is cold *out*"; "I want to *go out*"; "I have *a hat*"). Another miscue has some overlap with the words they replace in terms of both meaning (semantic cues) and letters (graphophonemic cues), but are not exact matches (*"Mommy"* for *"Mother"*). Taken together, these

ERIC'S MISCUES WHILE READING "WHAT WILL LITTLE BEAR WEAR?"

out
It is cold. ^
See the snow.
See the snow come down.

Mommy
Little Bear said, "Mother Bear,
I am cold.
See the snow.

go out
I want [something] to put on."

Mommy   *a hat*
So Mother Bear made something
for Little Bear.
"See, Little Bear," she said,

a hat
"I have something for my little bear.
Here it is.
"Put it on [your head]."
"Oh," said Little Bear,
"it is a hat. //
["Hurray! Now I will not be cold."
Little Bear went out to play.]

miscues indicate that Eric probably needs additional decoding practice so that his word recognition becomes increasingly accurate and automatic. He would also benefit from fluency-oriented instruction to consolidate this knowledge.

In terms of evaluating your students, it is important that your texts match your purposes (see Figure 3.3). If you are using the results as part of a broader evaluation (i.e., analyzing miscues or taking running records), you can select texts that are part of your curriculum, including content-area material. You can also use CBMs, since they also allow you to develop a sense of how fluent your students are when reading their actual classroom material (e.g., Madelaine & Wheldall, 1999, 2004). CBMs were originally designed as an alternative to norm-referenced tests. Importantly, a great deal of research has been undertaken using this procedure and, when implemented properly (i.e., using a consistent or standardized

TABLE 3.1. Oral Reading Fluency Target Rate Norms

Grade	Fall	Winter	Spring
1		10–30	30–60
2	30–60	50–80	70–100
3	50–90	70–100	80–110
4	70–110	80–120	100–140
5	80–120	100–140	110–150
6	100–140	110–150	120–160
7	110–150	120–160	130–170
8	120–160	130–170	140–180

Note. From Rasinski (2004b). Copyright by Pacific Resources for Education and Learning. Reprinted by permission.

protocol), they are considered "reliable and valid, quick and easy to administer repeatedly, inexpensive, unobtrusive, sensitive to small changes in progress, and able to be used to make instructional decisions" (Madelaine & Wheldall, 1999, p. 74). Despite these pluses, there are also some downsides to true CBMs, including the time required to identify passages for evaluation and the variability in reading levels between, and even within, selections.

One solution to the problems stemming from classroom-based CBMs has been the identification of passages that are unconnected to a specific curriculum, or selections that have not been designed for classroom use (Deno & Marston, 2006). DIBELS (Good & Kaminski, 2002) and AIMSweb (Shinn & Shinn, 2002) are widely used examples of such selections and represent the third assessment option. If you are undertaking an evaluation designated by your school or district, it is likely you will be using one of these widely available tests. In this case, your students will be expected to read from among the selections provided at a given grade level. Further, these assessments have a well-defined protocol for implementation and interpretation.

Options for measuring CWPM

Curriculum-based measures (CBMs) taken from classroom selections	Standardized selections (e.g., DIBELS, AIMSweb)

FIGURE 3.3. Choosing text for fluency assessments.

Remember, though, that these CBMs, like the evaluations you might create with your own classroom materials (whether using insertions or not), provide only a partial picture of fluency (Kuhn et al., 2010). Since students' CWPM can be measured without a corresponding measure of prosody, rate can end up being overemphasized at the expense of understanding; we have found this to be especially true when these assessments are used as high-stakes measures rather than for simply providing teachers with information about their learners. Additionally, when the passages are not connected with your curriculum, you may end up with a different sense of your students' ability than you would have found using material from the classroom. In both of these cases, it is possible to end up with a misidentification of your fluent and disfluent readers.

For example, if you rely exclusively on CWPM, you may fail to identify those students who are quick and accurate but who lack prosody (Kuhn et al., 2010). Further, it is possible that the procedure itself (especially when overemphasized) may leave your students with the false sense that reading should be developed for speed rather than meaning, an understanding that is highly problematic. Further, concentrating on rapid reading can actually interfere with comprehension by moving attention away from meaning toward word recognition. Finally, by teaching students to read for speed alone the measure being used can actually be invalidated.

The following example can help illustrate what we mean. According to Jan Hasbrouck and Gerald Tindal (2006), students at the 25th percentile in grade 2 read at 42 CWPM; since this measure is considered to be a proxy for overall reading ability, these students are considered to be reading below grade level. However, simply teaching these learners to read more quickly will not necessarily improve their overall reading ability. In fact, by focusing too heavily on rate, they may concentrate *less* on the construction of meaning. In this scenario, an increase in their CWPM may give your learners the appearance of improved reading ability, when in fact only their reading rate has changed. However, you can easily avoid these shortcomings by adopting a fuller understanding of fluency.

Assessing Prosodic Reading

The third component of fluent reading is prosody. And while it is as important to fluency as accuracy and automaticity, it has not received the same amount of attention (Kuhn et al., 2010). We believe there are several reasons for this problem. First, it is easy to evaluate students' reading rate; you can measure learners' CWPM quickly and accurately. Prosody, on the other hand, has to be measured qualitatively and is therefore more subjective. Next, automaticity and fluency have often been considered equivalent; in other words, learners who read quickly are often considered fluent. We disagree with this definition; while measuring reading rate helps to determine students' growth as skilled readers, it does not provide the whole picture.

Rather than establishing a goal of fast reading, we believe students should be developing the understanding that good oral reading incorporates many of the same components that exist in speech, including appropriate phrasing, stress, emphasis, *and* pacing (Kuhn et al., 2010). To ensure that our students' reading reflects those goals, we need to integrate these elements into our fluency instruction. And, since what we assess often indicates what we believe to be important, we also think it is important to assess prosody. Evaluating prosody is less precise than determining CWPM. This means whichever measure you choose, you will need to apply a greater degree of interpretation to your students' reading than is the case for the CWPM measures. However, your extra effort can be well worth it.

Several scales can help you assess the prosodic elements of your students' reading. The first, the National Assessment of Educational Progress (NAEP) Oral Reading Fluency Scale (1995), has the broadest classifications; it uses four categories to

NATIONAL ASSESSMENT OF EDUCATIONAL PROGRESS'S ORAL READING FLUENCY SCALE

Level 4

Reads primarily in larger, meaningful phrase groups. Although some regressions, repetitions and deviations from text may be present, those do not appear to detract from the overall structure of the story. Preservation of the author's syntax is consistent. Some or most of the story is read with expressive interpretation.

Level 3

Reads primarily in three- or four-word phrase groups. Some smaller groupings may be present. However, the majority of phrasing seems appropriate and preserves the syntax of the author. Little or no expressive interpretation is present.

Level 2

Reads primarily in two-word phrases with some three- or four-word groupings. Some word-by-word reading may be present. Word groupings may seem awkward and unrelated to larger context of sentence or passage.

Level 1

Reads primarily word-by-word. Occasionally two-word or three-word phrases may occur, but these are infrequent and/or they do not preserve meaningful syntax.

Note. From National Assessment of Educational Progress (1995).

MULTIDIMENSIONAL FLUENCY SCALE

Use the following scales to rate reader fluency on the dimensions of expression and volume, phrasing, smoothness, and pace.

A. Expression and Volume

1. Reads with little expression or enthusiasm in voice. Reads words as if simply to get them out. Little sense of trying to make text sound like natural language. Tends to read in a quiet voice.
2. Some expression. Begins to use voice to make text sound like natural language in some areas of the text, but not others. Focus remains largely on saying the words. Still reads in a voice that is quiet.
3. Sounds like natural language throughout the better part of the passage. Occasionally slips into expressionless reading. Voice volume is generally appropriate throughout the text.
4. Reads with good expression and enthusiasm throughout the text. Sounds like natural language. The reader is able to vary expression and volume to match his/her interpretation of the passage.

B. Phrasing

1. Monotonic with little sense of phrase boundaries, frequent word-by-word reading.
2. Frequent two and three word phrases giving the impression of choppy reading; improper stress and intonation that fail to mark ends of sentences and clauses.
3. Mixture of run-ons, mid-sentence pauses for breath, and possibly some choppiness; reasonable stress/intonation.
4. Generally well-phrased, mostly in clause and sentence units, with adequate attention to expression.

C. Smoothness

1. Frequent extended pauses, hesitations, false starts, sound-outs, repetitions, and/or multiple attempts.
2. Several "rough spots" in text where extended pauses, hesitations, etc., are more frequent and disruptive.
3. Occasional breaks in smoothness caused by difficulties with specific words and/or structures.
4. Generally smooth reading with some breaks, but word and structure difficulties are resolved quickly, usually through self-correction.

D. Pace (during sections of minimal disruption)

1. Slow and laborious.
2. Moderately slow.
3. Uneven mixture of fast and slow reading.
4. Consistently conversational.

Note. From Rasinski (2004b). Copyright by Pacific Resources for Education and Learning. Reprinted by permission.

describe oral reading, which also makes it the easiest to implement. The second scale, created by Richard Allington and Steven Brown (Allington, 1983), is slightly more nuanced. It incorporates six categories, rather than four; as such, it is somewhat more refined in the areas of punctuation and expression. The Multidimensional Fluency Scale (Rasinski, 2004b) is the most detailed of the commonly used scales. It incorporates four distinct dimensions of prosody, expression and volume, phrasing, smoothness, and pace, and defines four categories within each. This level of detail makes its use more complex and time-consuming. However, with four categories across four dimensions, it allows you to observe finer degrees of change in your students' prosody.

Be on the lookout for more assessments of prosody. The most recent scale, the Comprehensive Oral Reading Fluency Scale (CORFS; Benjamin et al., 2013), is based on spectrographic analysis of actual oral readings. This analysis provides a visual "fingerprint" of what is being read "by generating a visual graphic representation of the features of speech (e.g., pitch, intensity, duration) that vary over time and can be measured for change directly" (p. 106). This process allows categories to be established using prosodic characteristics that were documented visually: intonation and pausing. According to the scale's creators, "intonation is defined as the rise and fall of pitch when speaking, usually used to convey meaning and importance" and "pausing can be defined as a complete absence of vocalizing as well as breaks in text from repetitions, hesitations, and prearticulations" (p. 131). These two components are coupled with a CWPM rating to create a global fluency score.

While the CORF scale has been field-tested by professionals who were trained to use it, it has not yet been evaluated for use in classrooms; therefore, we don't yet know how practical it will be. However, given that it is a multistep process, it seems reasonable to assume it would be somewhat more time-consuming than either the NAEP (1995) or the Allington and Brown (Allington, 1983) scales. On the other hand, with two categories instead of four, it would also seem likely that it would be less time-intensive than the Multidimensional Fluency Scale (Rasinski, 2004b).

To understand better how evaluation of prosody works, let's examine a specific example using the NAEP Oral Reading Fluency Scale (1995; p. 35). The scale looks at students' reading in terms of pace, smoothness, phrasing, and expression, and ranges from reading at the most basic level (Level 1, primarily word-by-word and lacking in expression) to the most advanced level (Level 4, reading that is expressive and incorporates both appropriate phrasing and pacing). In terms of general reading development based on grade-level texts, most of your first graders will be reading at Level 1 for the first half of the year. And, as they progress through the second half of first grade and into second and third grade, they should move through Levels 2, 3, and 4. By the fourth grade (and beyond), we should expect students who are reading at grade level to remain at Level 4.

If you agree with us that the NAEP scale is worth using in your classroom, we strongly recommend that you make an audio recording of your students' reading, at least until you are comfortable with the rating system. Recording your students' oral reading has a second advantage; it allows you to confirm their reading rates and miscues by referring back to the audio recording. If you choose to use the NAEP scale, the guidelines are quite self-explanatory, but it is important to consider the bulk of the reading when deciding whether to assign a student, say, a 2 or 3. In other words, if the student primarily reads using three- or four-word phrasing, then they should be rated a 3. Similarly, if the student is generally expressive, they should be rated a 4. Since there are often short deviations in children's reading, it is important to base your rating on the greater part of the selection.

It is also critical to remember that reading development is not a lockstep progression (e.g., McKenna & Stahl, 2009). Since children's reading development varies, you will find that some of your students will achieve these prosody levels earlier than others. On the other hand, you may notice some of your students have difficulty developing their prosody. In this case, it may be necessary to provide additional fluency instruction for these students. This may involve small-group lessons using some of the approaches presented in Chapter 6 while the rest of your students work on other aspects of their literacy development.

Finally, since determining students' prosody ratings is somewhat subjective (Benjamin et al., 2013), it is possible that your evaluation of a student's oral reading will differ to some extent from that of your colleagues. Given this, it is important to think about whether you want to work independently and maintain your own ratings or work with your peers to establish a consensus across classrooms. Either way, you might want to record several students reading a selection of passages to establish a protocol for rating your learners. We hope that this discussion has provided you with the confidence that a prosody rating is a worthwhile tool for integration into your assessment portfolio.

What about Informal Reading Inventories?

You may notice that we have not advocated for the use of informal reading inventories (IRIs) as fluency assessments per se. We are not recommending that you use IRIs because they are very time-consuming. Instead, we think that the use of CWPM and prosody should allow you to gauge how comfortable your students are with grade-level material. Additionally, this approach will allow you to evaluate your students at multiple points throughout the school year without spending significant amounts of time either preparing testing material or disrupting the flow of your classroom.

Conclusion

Given the multifaceted nature of fluency, we feel that the use of one of the available prosody scales, in conjunction with a CWPM rating, will provide you with a clearer understanding of your students' fluency development than could be achieved using a CWPM rating alone. And since both can be completed relatively quickly, it makes sense to use them together. However, we recommend recording students' oral reading whenever possible to establish greater confidence, and a higher level of accuracy, in your results. By affording yourself this additional information, you will have a better sense of the appropriateness of fluency instruction for your students as well as what form that instruction should take.

CHAPTER 4

• • • • • • • • • • •

Fluency Instruction
for Any Setting

GUIDING QUESTIONS

• •

- How are echo, choral, and partner readings similar and different?
- How do these approaches differ from round-robin reading (or the related approaches such as popcorn, popsicle, or combat reading)?
- How can these approaches help students access challenging texts?
- How can you create variation in your choral reading procedures?
- What types of student pairings are most effective for partner reading? Why?

Carolyn is a second-grade teacher struggling to meet the literacy needs of her students. They are a bright and inquisitive bunch, but half of them are not quite reading at the district's benchmark level. In addition, her administrators have undertaken several inservice presentations on the CCSS and are encouraging teachers to use "complex texts" during their literacy lessons. Her dilemma is figuring out how to use such texts when not all her students are reading grade-level material successfully.

Using Instructional Strategies
to Help Students Access Texts

• •

In order for students to become fluent readers, they need to spend time reading connected text (e.g., Kuhn et al., 2010). It is this practice that helps them develop automaticity and prosody, which, in turn, leads to greater fluency across all their reading. Many teachers continue with the old-fashioned practice of round-robin reading (Ash, Kuhn, & Walpole, 2009), a turn-taking routine where individual students read small portions of text aloud. We know that round-robin reading does not provide students with enough practice reading connected text for them to develop their fluency. Unfortunately, none of the popular oral reading routines developed to improve round-robin reading (e.g., popcorn reading, combat reading, popsicle reading) are any more effective than the approach they replace. The bottom line is that each child reads too little text. On the other hand, many of the more participatory routines, such as guided reading (Fountas & Pinnell, 1999), are designed specifically for instructional-level material; however, if we are to help our students become proficient under the CCSS, we need to introduce them to more complex texts as well (Common Core State Standards Initiative, 2012).

In this chapter, we present three research-based instructional strategies that can help your students transition to fluent reading while reading material that would otherwise be too challenging for them (Kuhn, 2009). Each of the strategies embraces Rasinski's (1989) principles for effective fluency instruction and supports your learners as they broaden their vocabulary and conceptual knowledge (Hirsch, 2003).

The three instructional strategies—echo reading, choral reading, and partner reading—can be used in a variety of settings and are foundational for several of the other routines introduced later in this book (Kuhn, 2009). We present these approaches according to the level of support that they offer (see Figure 4.1), starting with the strategy that provides the greatest amount of scaffolding for your students: echo reading.

Echo Reading

Echo reading is a teacher-assisted oral reading strategy that includes both teacher modeling and participation by all of your students (Kuhn, 2009). During echo

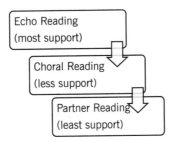

FIGURE 4.1. Basic fluency strategies in order of support provided (most to least).

MORE THAN JUST ROUND ROBIN:
THE HISTORY OF ORAL READING IN U.S. EDUCATION

Oral reading's role in the school curriculum has varied across the history of the United States (Rasinski & Hoffman, 2003). Early on, the majority of jobs did not require high levels of literacy; as a result formal schooling was often minimal. Additionally, since producing reading materials was quite costly, they were not plentiful. This combination meant that most individuals had low levels of literacy, and those individuals who could read well were often called upon by their fellow citizens to read aloud—either to share information (e.g., reading pamphlets to citizens during the Revolutionary War) or to entertain or enlighten (e.g., reading Bible tracts at home). As a result, much literacy instruction was geared toward oral reading, and there was a significant emphasis on personal interpretations of a given text (Hoffman & Crone, 1985). For example, if several students were assigned to read a monologue from *Much Ado about Nothing*, each student's use of prosodic elements could make for a highly personal and much more entertaining interpretation of the piece.

Over the course of the 20th century, however, two things changed: workers were required to achieve higher levels of literacy and written materials became significantly cheaper to produce. As a result, a far higher percentage of the population became literate, and individuals began reading more often, across a much wider range of material, and for their own purposes. This shift was also reflected in the schools' literacy curriculum as silent reading began to replace oral reading as the main form of instruction. Unfortunately, silent reading comes with its own difficulties. For example, when learners are reading silently, it is impossible to know how much progress they are making or even if they are engaging with the text. In order for teachers to determine how well students were reading, it was necessary to ask students to read aloud periodically. Eventually, randomly checking students' reading came to be seen as a way to ensure that each student spent some of their time reading, that difficult material was covered, and that students were engaged (Kuhn, 2014). As a result, the practice of *round-robin reading* (or the corresponding practices of popcorn, popsicle, and combat reading), in which individual children take turns reading short segments of text aloud, became a mainstay of the curriculum—a practice that continues in far too many classrooms today.

The critiques of round-robin reading approaches are many (e.g., Kuhn, Ash, & Gregory, 2012). To begin with, reading a paragraph or two aloud each day does not provide students with nearly enough practice to develop their reading skills. And, while using these methods may allow you to "cover" the material at hand, they actually make comprehension more difficult by taking a unified text and breaking it up into smaller—and harder to follow—parts. Finally, these approaches fail to engage learners. For example, students who are skilled readers become bored when their less skilled peers are reading, whereas striving readers are often embarrassed by their lack of skill and simply hope to get the process over and done with as quickly as possible. Fortunately, there are a number of effective alternatives presented throughout this book that can contribute to the reading development of your students. We believe they will provide you with useful approaches that can be easily integrated into your classroom while being far more beneficial than those you are replacing.

> ## RASINSKI'S PRINCIPLES OF EFFECTIVE FLUENCY INSTRUCTION
>
> - Principle 1—Children should hear **models of good oral reading**. This allows your students to focus on the meaning of the text without overly focusing on the individual words.
> - Principle 2—Teachers should provide **oral support and assistance for students** as they make the transition to fluent reading. Echo, choral, and partner reading provide that support and give your students a chance to hear a fluent, expressive reading of the text.
> - Principle 3—**Practice** is the key to fluency development. The time spent practicing is essential to helping students automatize their word recognition (Samuels, 2004) and will lead to them becoming more fluent readers.
> - Principle 4—Instruction should focus on **appropriate phrasing**. Fluent readers chunk the words in text into appropriate phrases that help to convey meaning. The ability to separate text into such phrasing aids comprehension.

reading, your children spend significantly more time reading connected text than they would with any of the versions of round-robin reading (e.g., popcorn, popsicle; Ash et al., 2009); instead of spending much of their reading time waiting for their turn, students are instead engaged in practice. Implementing echo reading involves you reading a section of text aloud as your students follow along silently in their own copies, perhaps even tracking what you are reading with their index finger (Kuhn, 2009). The students then reread the same section aloud in unison. Echo reading provides students with support through your fluent, expressive modeling. In other words, your reading supplies a model of accurate word reading, pacing, and inflection that your students can immediately use. Their echoing back gives them an opportunity to practice the fluent reading you just modeled. Whether you read along with your students as they echo depends on your goals; if you want to provide them with additional support and pacing, it makes sense for you to read along again. If, on the other hand, you want to hear how they are reading, then you should let them read on their own.

Echo reading is ideal for an initial presentation of a text that students will reread later or for the use of more challenging texts with that same group (Kuhn, 2009). It is the high degree of scaffolding involved in echo reading that makes more complex texts accessible. Therefore, it doesn't make sense to use echo reading with texts that are easy for students to read; however, it does make perfect sense to use it with the type of challenging material required by the CCSS (Common Core State Standards Initiative, 2012). A broad range of texts can be used effectively with echo reading, including selections from core program anthologies, trade books, content-area textbooks, or even supplemental material from magazines or the Internet (Kuhn, 2009). When using this procedure, some teachers choose to read the entire text aloud to their class and undertake comprehension and vocabulary activities before starting the echo procedure. This is one way to ensure that oral reading practice will not be sidetracked by misunderstandings related to comprehension. However, either version has been shown to be successful in the classroom (Kuhn & Schwanenflugel, 2008).

When children are learning to echo-read (Kuhn, 2009), they need to understand that they are active participants during your modeling as well as when they are reading aloud. In order to do this, they need to follow along with your initial reading. You may find moving around the room as you read a useful way to monitor their attention to the text. You will also want to make sure that everyone is literally on the same page and can point to the place where you are going to begin before you start reading.

When first introducing the procedure, it is often helpful to practice with short pieces of text to confirm that your students understand their responsibilities (Kuhn, 2009). They can begin practicing by echoing a few sentences at a time. It may take several attempts at these "short echoes" before they understand what they are supposed to do. However, once they have this down, it is important that you should increase the length of the selections to prevent students from using their auditory memory to echo what you have read. For the most part, this can be achieved in several sessions. And when you first start practicing with your students, it may be helpful to join your students as they echo the sentences back to you. This additional support can be faded as your students develop an understanding of the procedure.

Once the instructional strategy is fully implemented, your students should be able to echo longer and more complex pieces of text with fluency (Kuhn, 2009). Your goal is for the students to echo your reading of several paragraphs or even a page (depending on the amount of text on a page and your students' reading ability). And since comprehension is always the goal of proficient reading, you'll want to clarify any confusions, explain vocabulary, and check for understanding as you work your way through the text. As your students become increasingly fluent, you will likely reduce your use of echo reading or save it for texts that you feel would really benefit from the high level of support it provides.

Echo Reading in Action

- Supply each student with his own copy of the text to use as you echo.

- Have all students point to the first word on the first page before you begin. Check that all students are ready to start.

- Monitor students' engagement with the text while you are reading and while they are echoing by circulating around the room.

- Before full implementation of the procedure, you'll want to practice with short pieces of text. Gradually increase the amount of text that the students echo.

Choral Reading

Choral reading is another teacher-assisted oral reading strategy in which you and your students simultaneously read a text or a section of text aloud (Kuhn, 2009). It incorporates less support than echo reading, but still provides students with a model for developing automaticity and prosody. It is sometimes used as a follow-up to echo reading of challenging texts, providing students with another opportunity to work with the material. However, since choral reading provides less scaffolding, using it after echo reading moves the student toward greater independence. That continuum, referred to as the gradual-release-of-responsibility model (e.g., Pearson & Gallagher, 1983), describes the process through which teachers move students from assisted to independent performance of skills (see Figure 4.2).

Choral reading can also be used with texts at your students' instructional level if your goal is to work on pacing or expression (Kuhn, 2009). For that purpose, you may want to use a poem, a speech, or a highly descriptive passage to read chorally. Your students may be able to decode most or all of the words in these texts, but choral reading can provide them with an opportunity to read with better pacing or expression—both worthwhile goals for your instructional time. The time that your students spend working on these skills can translate into better pacing and expression when they read independently.

As with echo reading, all students in a choral-reading session need their own copies of the text (Kuhn, 2009). You should explain to the students that you are all going to read the text together and that their job is to mimic you. In other words, their reading should sound like yours in terms of pacing, inflection, and tone. You

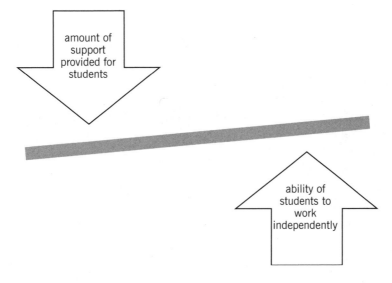

FIGURE 4.2. Gradual release of responsibility.

may want to begin by practicing on a short poem or a brief passage from a longer selection. You should also read a bit more slowly and with greater emphasis than you normally would, at least for the first few times, until students understand the procedure. Ultimately, however, your reading should be lively and reflect the mood of the text but should not be overly exaggerated or slower than your normal read-alouds.

When you are using choral reading specifically for pacing and expression, introducing variations may keep it fun and increase your students' interest in the strategy (Kuhn, 2009). You may want to choose poems written for two voices and divide the class into two groups for the reading (see the list of poems for multiple voices below for examples). You can divide your class by splitting the group in half using an alphabetized list of their names or have them count off by twos. Another fun variation on choral reading is to have children read the parts of

BOOKS WITH POEMS FOR MULTIPLE VOICES

You Read to Me, I'll Read to You by John Ciardi (1962)

Big Talk: Poems for Four Voices by Paul Fleischman (2008)

I Am Phoenix: Poems for Two Voices by Paul Fleischman (1985)

Joyful Noise: Poems for Two Voices by Paul Fleischman (2004)

Messing Around on the Monkey Bars: And Other School Poems for Two Voices by Betsy Franco (2009)

Seeds, Bees, Butterflies and More!: Poems for Two Voices by Carole Gerber (2013)

You Read to Me, I'll Read to You: Very Short Fables to Read Together by Mary Ann Hoberman (2013)

You Read to Me, I'll Read to You: Very Short Fairy Tales to Read Together by Mary Ann Hoberman (2012)

You Read to Me, I'll Read to You: Very Short Mother Goose Tales to Read Together by Mary Ann Hoberman (2012)

You Read to Me, I'll Read to You: Very Short Scary Tales to Read Together by Mary Ann Hoberman (2009)

You Read to Me, I'll Read to You: Very Short Stories to Read Together by Mary Ann Hoberman (2006)

You Read to Me, I'll Read to You: Very Short Tall Tales to Read Together by Mary Ann Hoberman (2014)

Math Talk: Mathematical Ideas in Poems for Two Voices by Theoni Pappas (1993)

You Read to Me and I'll Read to You: Stories to Share from the 20th Century by Janet Schulman (2001)

different characters in voices that evoke those characters. Young characters can have high-pitched voices, older characters can have shakier, weaker voices, and scary characters can have a spooky, menacing quality to their voices.

Again, it is important that you walk around the room to monitor your students' engagement with the text (Kuhn, 2009). Some students may struggle to keep pace with you or may "mumble read." You can support those students by standing close to them and pointing to the words as you read them. These learners need particular help staying focused on and engaged with the text if the choral reading is to benefit them. Finally, you should introduce and clarify challenging vocabulary and discuss the material since you want your students to understand what they are reading and not just imitate your reading without comprehension.

Choral Reading in Action

• Supply each student with her own copy of the text. Make sure each student knows where to begin on the page.

• Explain the procedure to the class by letting them know they are going to mimic you and try to come as close as possible to your pacing and expression as you read.

• You can begin practicing the procedure by using a short poem or passage and reading at a slightly slower pace than normal. This will help your students succeed with the procedure and build their confidence for longer passages.

• Move around the room as you read and monitor your students' engagement with the text. Students must have their eyes on the words.

• Read loud enough so that all students can hear your voice above the group. Use your voice to make the text come alive!

Partner Reading

The last strategy introduced in this chapter is partner reading (Meisinger & Bradley, 2008). This is not a teacher-assisted approach, but one in which your students work in partnerships to support each other. This approach significantly increases the amount of reading that your students can accomplish in a given period. The students are not waiting for their turn to read among a group of 25, but rather are reading in a partnership of two. Quite a difference in the amount of reading time undertaken by each student in the class!

In partner reading (Meisinger & Bradley, 2008), one student is the reader and the other student is the listener/supporter. After each page (or less if needed) is read, the roles switch and the reader becomes the listener and the listener becomes the reader. The reader's job is to read aloud in a clear, expressive voice while the listener follows along and attends to what the partner is reading. If the reader runs into any difficulty, the listener is there to provide support. This support can consist of helping with misread words, providing unknown words, helping the reader remember word-reading strategies already taught, finding the place in text, and being positive and encouraging. Your students should be familiar with this kind of support having seen you provide it in your own instruction, but you may want to provide them with specific guidance through demonstration lessons.

Partner reading is motivating for students since they have the opportunity to work together. The social aspect of partner reading makes it a very popular instructional strategy. However, if a text is challenging, it is best used as a follow-up approach once your students have developed some familiarity with the material through echo or choral reading. Alternatively, it can be used when your students are reading a text that is less challenging, one closer to their instructional level.

Given that partner reading is not a teacher-led approach, your students will need you to spend more time teaching and practicing the procedure so that they are equipped to work with their partner (Meisinger & Bradley, 2008). When first practicing, students should switch roles each paragraph or two in order to develop greater stamina. With continued practice, they will be able to stretch to reading a full page for each turn. During these practice sessions, you will want to model partner-reading behaviors. Your students should be encouraged to use quiet voices when they read. A fun way to teach that is by having volunteers demonstrate reading voices that are too loud, too soft, and just right (the "Goldilocks voice"). They should then be taught a partner-reading position, in which two students sit next to each other, virtually "shoulder to shoulder." Positive support and encouragement should also be modeled. It may be helpful at this point to demonstrate the right way and the wrong way to give a partner support (e.g., "That word is pronounced *about*," instead of "You're kidding! You don't know that word?"). Students should know the places in your room that are open spaces for partner reading. These can include floor space, desks, classroom nooks, or any space that is comfortable for the students and can be monitored by you.

Your role during partner reading is to circulate throughout the classroom, making sure all partners are focused and on task (Meisinger & Bradley, 2008). You should also be available to provide assistance when needed. That support can take the form of working with students on a word that neither partner can figure out, coaching a student on how to be a helpful partner as the reading is taking place, resolving disputes between partners who find this kind of independent partner work initially challenging, or simply listening to the pairs of students as they read aloud.

Partners can be self-selected or chosen by you (Meisinger & Bradley, 2008). Self-selected partners may be motivating for your students. However, since the most beneficial partnerships are those where pairs read across reading levels, it is possible that self-selected partners may fail to include this feature. A simple way to create partnerships across reading levels is to rank your readers from the highest to lowest and list the students in that order (e.g., Fuchs & Fuchs, 1998; Strickland, Ganske, & Monroe, 2002). Split the list in half and then place the first name from the second list next to the first name on the first list and so forth (see Figure 4.3). In this way, your highest reader will be partnered with an average reader and your lowest reader will also be partnered with an average reader. This is the ideal arrangement since reading levels that are too far apart can lead to frustration for both partners. Similarly, if two of your lowest readers are partnered, they may not be able to give each other enough support to make the partnership fruitful. On the other hand, if two of your highest readers are placed together, the selections may not provide enough challenge for them to benefit from each other's support or to keep them engaged throughout the activity.

Within each pair, students should be labeled Student A and Student B. Alternative days can be "A days" and "B days." On "A days," Student A can read first, and on "B days," Student B can read first (Meisinger & Bradley, 2008). In this way, no single partner gets to be the first reader every day.

Finally, it is critical that your students remain engaged throughout the partner-reading sessions (Meisinger & Bradley, 2008). Students should know that if they finish reading the text before the end of the session, they should start reading the selection again. However, this time the second partner should start the reading and each student should read the opposite pages from their first reading.

Skill rank	Name	Skill rank	Name
1	Luis	11	Grover
2	Shrya	12	Desiree
3	Salvador	13	Gabriella
4	Shaquine	14	Albert
5	Olivia	15	Ingrid
6	Amelia	16	Leo
7	Daniel	17	Gregory
8	Harshul	18	Ria
9	Jacob	19	J. J.
10	Thomas	20	Chloe

FIGURE 4.3. Example of a classroom partner-reading list.

Partner Reading in Action

- Each student should have his or her own copy of the text to work with.

- Discuss and model the roles of each partner before starting.

- Have your students practice the procedure with each student reading only a paragraph or two before switching roles. Eventually partners should be able to read multiple paragraphs or even a page at a time depending on the level of text and your readers' abilities. Remind students that if a sentence continues across a page they should complete the sentence on the new page.

- Partnerships should be formed across reading levels to ensure that both partners get the most out of the activity.

- Monitor and support partners throughout the activity by circulating around the room and helping students with both reading and management issues.

Conclusion

Echo, choral, and partner reading are three easy-to-implement, effective fluency approaches that can be used in a variety of situations within your classroom. These procedures can help you promote fluency while introducing your students to challenging texts, a critical aspect of their effective preparation under the CCSS. It is also worth noting that these strategies are integrated into several other fluency-oriented instructional approaches featured in later chapters and are important methods for broader reading development in an early elementary classroom.

CHAPTER 5

Fluency Instruction for Shared Reading

GUIDING QUESTIONS

- How are independent, instructional, and frustration reading levels traditionally defined?
- How do the shared reading approaches discussed in this chapter provide students with access to challenging texts?
- What are the similarities and differences between Fluency-Oriented Reading Instruction and Wide Fluency-Oriented Reading Instruction?
- What are the benefits of each approach?
- How can you select appropriate material for these approaches to shared reading?

Kwame is a new teacher who learned about matching texts to learners during his undergraduate teacher preparation program. However, he is finding that adhering to a strict definition of an instructional reading level does not always meet the needs of his students. During guided reading the definitions for independent, instructional, and frustration reading levels seem to work, but during shared reading or when a student's motivation is very high, some of his students are able to benefit from texts that his former professors would have said were too hard. Should he stick with a strict interpretation of reading levels or go with his blossoming experience in this area?

Selecting Appropriate Texts

It is important to provide your students with texts that will help them move forward in acquiring their reading skills. Traditionally, we thought that we could best do this by matching books and readers; this process involved determining each student's instructional reading level and making sure that they maximized the amount of time spent reading at that level. This framework was originally proposed by Emmet Betts in the 1940s (Betts, 1946). He identified an independent level, an instructional level, and a frustration level (see Figure 5.1). According to Betts, students who read at the independent level can decode between 99 and 100% of the words in a passage and their comprehension is between 90 and 100%. They are at an instructional level when their decoding is between 95 and 98% and their comprehension is between 75 and 89%. Frustration level includes any text in which less than 90% of the text is correctly decoded or comprehension is below 50%. It is important to remember that Betts's framework was developed using the typical instructional format of the time. That format involved the teacher working with several small groups of readers. Each group was provided with background information and vocabulary support for the material they were reading. The children then engaged in a round-robin reading of the story, which was followed by questions, discussion, and skills activities (McKenna & Stahl, 2009).

However, for the kind of shared reading activities that will be introduced in this chapter, Betts's framework simply doesn't apply. Shared reading allows teachers to teach reading strategies with a group of students, often the entire class, using a common or shared text (Holdaway, 1979). While finding an instructional level may be helpful for the guided reading portion of your literacy instruction, the increased scaffolding and support provided during the shared reading approaches presented in this chapter allow you to use higher levels of text with your readers. In fact, research has shown that it is important to use more challenging text during fluency instruction—as long as you provide sufficient support for your readers (Kuhn & Schwanenflugel, 2006; Stahl & Heubach, 2005). Your students need

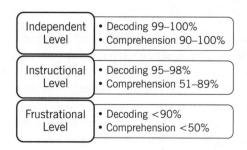

FIGURE 5.1. Betts's reading level framework.

to be using material that is at least at their grade level during the shared reading activities that follow. The structure and support of the two approaches introduced on the following pages will help even those students who are reading below grade level to read the material successfully by the end of the week. And by the end of the year, your students' independent reading skills should improve as a consequence of the increased time they spend reading challenging connected text.

In this chapter, we introduce two research-based fluency approaches that can be used with your entire class during the shared reading portion of your literacy instruction. The first of these, Fluency-Oriented Reading Instruction (FORI; Stahl & Heubach, 2005), incorporates the use of repetition while the second, Wide Fluency-Oriented Reading Instruction (Wide FORI; Kuhn et al., 2006), uses multiple scaffolded texts. These approaches were designed for second and third graders who are making the transition to fluent reading, but can be used with any students who are at this point in their reading development. Both approaches maintain a focus on comprehension early in the weekly lesson plan, as well as provide a model of fluent, expressive reading. Before presenting these methods, however, we want to discuss the effectiveness of the two underlying instructional approaches, repeated reading and scaffolded wide reading.

Repeated versus Scaffolded Wide Reading

Jay Samuels's (1979) influential article describing automaticity theory and fluency instruction argued that many of the students having difficulties with automatic word recognition were simply not provided with enough exposure to their reading material. In fact, they only read a given text once before moving on to a new selection. Samuels recommended having these students reread a text several times in order to develop enough familiarity with the material to read it automatically. Over the past three decades, this approach has proven effective in helping students develop both their reading rate and their accuracy. As a result, repetition has become an underlying tenet of many of the instructional methods designed to increase fluency (Dowhower, 1989; National Institute of Child Health and Human Development, 2000). However, in a review of fluency instruction that examined dozens of studies (Kuhn & Stahl, 2003), students who read texts repeatedly and those who read equivalent amounts of nonrepeated, but scaffolded, texts appeared to make equivalent gains. This led to the question of whether it was the repetition per se that was the key to the development of fluency or if time spent reading connected text in a nonrepetitive format was just as effective when support and scaffolding were provided.

Several studies published since the Kuhn and Stahl (2003) review have shown that wide reading is not only as effective as repeated reading in developing several critical components of fluency (accurate and automatic word recognition, text comprehension, prosody), but may actually be more effective since learning a given word may be easier when you see it in a variety of contexts. Since there is a high degree of overlap among words in elementary-level texts, if you simply provide students with access to lots of texts, you are increasing their chances of encountering the same words in multiple contexts. The two approaches presented in this chapter, FORI and Wide FORI, are designed to address fluency instruction during shared reading and to ensure your students encounter a range of words multiple times. Your decision regarding which of the approaches you use may hinge on the amount of appropriate reading material available to you. However, later in this chapter we also discuss ways you can increase the number of selections available to your students without having to buy entire-class sets of books.

Fluency-Oriented Reading Instruction

FORI is a whole-group approach originally developed for use in a district that had mandated all students to be taught exclusively with grade-level texts. This mandate was put into place despite the concerns of teachers whose classrooms included many students who were not reading at grade level. Since the teachers and researchers developing the approach didn't want to set students up for failure, they included extensive amounts of scaffolding in the lesson plans. Their goal was to make sure the materials were accessible to all of the students in the classroom. This involved providing heavily scaffolded instruction using material that was repeated several times over the course of a week. Remember that within a gradual-release-of-responsibility model (Pearson & Gallagher, 1983; see Figure 4.2 in Chapter 4) the goal is for teacher scaffolding to be reduced gradually so that the students will be able to read the grade-level text independently by the end of the week.

Teachers in the original FORI study used a commercial core program, but the approach has been replicated since using literature anthologies as well as trade books. Successful implementation is dependent on your use of grade-level material, but it doesn't matter whether that material takes the form of an anthology selection, a content-area textbook, or a trade book. Importantly, in the initial 2-year study (Stahl & Heubach, 2005), children on average saw growth on the Qualitative Reading Inventory (Leslie & Caldwell, 1995) of 1 year 8 months in the first year and 1 year 7 months in the second year.

FORI has a straightforward, 5-day lesson plan that is easy to implement. However, it is *essential* that students read connected text for 20–30 minutes each day for the program to be implemented successfully, so poems and other short selections are not sufficient to achieve the desired results. And since your students need to spend substantial amounts of time engaged with text for their word recognition to become automatic, if you don't have sufficiently long selections available in your classroom, you may need to dig out some old anthologies from your school's storage closets to expand the number of readings available for your lessons.

While the 5-day lesson plan may look very simple, we caution you that when teachers haven't paid enough attention to text length, time on task, or purposeful implementation of the procedure, the approach has not been effective. However, with thoughtful and purposeful implementation, students will be able to read texts that would otherwise be deemed too difficult for them, thereby giving you a wonderful opportunity to teach higher-level vocabulary and concepts, a factor that is also critical to success with the CCSS. Students who have also participated in FORI classrooms enjoyed the regularity of the procedure, and the structure of the method reduces the pressure to create entirely new lesson plans each week.

FORI IN ACTION: WEEKLY LESSON PLAN

	Monday	Tuesday	Wednesday	Thursday	Friday
FORI daily classroom plans	• Teacher introduces the selection to the class using pre-reading activities. • Teacher reads the selection to the class while the class follows in their individual copies. • Teacher leads discussion of the selection to keep the focus on comprehension.	• Teacher and students echo-read the story • Comprehension strategies should be infused throughout the selection (student questioning, vocabulary work, etc.).	• Teacher and students choral-read the selection.	• Students partner-read the selection.	• Students complete extension activities to broaden comprehension of text. • Activities may include student-led discussions, written responses, construction of charts and diagrams, etc.
Home reading	• Students read for 20–30 minutes a book of their own choosing.	• Students take home target selection and read it to a friend or family member.	• Students who need more practice read the target selection; others read a selection of their own choosing.	• Students who need more practice read the target selection; others read a selection of their own choosing.	• Students read a book of their own choosing for 20–30 minutes.

FORI in Action

Day 1: Introducing the Text

The first day begins with an introduction of the text for the week. This introduction can include a variety of preteaching activities including making predictions, building vocabulary, and activating prior knowledge. In fact, you can use activities for a given text during other parts of your literacy instruction. For example, if a story is set in a particular foreign country, you might introduce information about that country, show it on a map or globe, and even talk about customs and foods of that country. You could then link this to a text you are reading as part of your social studies curriculum.

Once you have introduced the text with some preteaching activities, you should read the entire text aloud while the students follow along in their own copies. While you are reading, you should be circulating around the room making sure all your students are following along. Your fluent reading of the text will not only serve as a model for your students, it allows them to hear and experience the entire story before being required to read it themselves. Your students can see the words as they are being pronounced without dealing with the demands of having to decode the words themselves; at the same time, students are given the opportunity to experience the selection as a whole.

Next, you'll want to lead a discussion about the text you just read. You can emphasize plot ("What happened after the boy got home?"), character ("Why did she decide to do that?"), setting ("Why did the author choose to have the story take place in a park?"), or any other comprehension questions that will make clear to the students that the goal of reading is the construction of meaning. This is an essential part of the first day's lesson. For young children, who spend a great deal of time and energy on word recognition, it's important that you don't leave them with the impression that reading is about "getting the words right." Your attention to comprehension at the earliest phases of reading reinforces the idea that reading is about understanding the text. For homework, children read a book of their own choosing.

Day 2: Echo Reading

On the second day, you will conduct an echo reading of the text by reading a section of text and then having the class read that piece of text back to you. If this is the first time you have echo-read with your students, you can start with small chunks for them to echo—perhaps just a sentence or two. Within a few weeks, they will be able to echo larger chunks of text—at least a paragraph or two at a time. It is important that you work toward echoing larger chunks of text to ensure that your students aren't relying on auditory memory. By using larger chunks, you are forcing your students to attend to the text as it is written rather than trying to remember what they heard you say. Eventually you may be able to echo as much as an entire page as long as your students are comfortable and the layout of the page is not too overwhelming. During the echo reading, you should be circulating throughout the room monitoring your students' reading.

Just like you did on Day 1, you should also maintain a focus on comprehension, and not exclusively on word recognition. You can do this by interspersing questions intermittently to check on vocabulary and comprehension. After completing the reading, you may either have pairs of students take turns summarizing the passage or have individuals undertake written responses. In fact, any grade-appropriate comprehension activity that keeps the students focused on the meaning of the text would be appropriate. Students' at-home reading of the text starts with their homework on Day 2. They should now be comfortable enough with the text (after two in-school readings) to read it on their own or with limited help at home and should read the selection to a family member or friend.

Day 3: Choral Reading

The third day of the week is the shortest day of instruction for you and your students since it consists of reading the selection chorally. As you read with the class, you'll again want to circulate throughout the room, paying particular attention to those students who may be having trouble keeping up with the reading and refocusing those who have lost their place. You may also want to have those students who are most likely to struggle sit near students whom you are confident will provide a good model.

The homework for Day 3 should be tailored to the needs of your students. Students who are fairly comfortable reading the passage can read something of their own choosing for homework. Students who are still in need of practice on the week's text should read it again to a family member or friend at home.

Day 4: Partner Reading

The final rereading of the text for the week is done with a partner. The class should be divided into pairs of readers (see Chapter 4 for strategies for matching partners) with each partner reading alternating pages. When the reader gets to the bottom of a page, she or he should finish any sentence or paragraph that she or he starts, even if it goes onto the next page. Since the group has already read this material at least three times, students should be able to provide one another with support and coaching if their partners experience difficulty.

If partners find there is extra time after the first reading of the text, they should start rereading by switching pages for the second round. Homework is again differentiated according to the needs of your students. Those who are reading the text fluently can choose their own text to read for homework; those who need more practice should read the week's text one more time.

Day 5: Extension Activities

The last day of the week is devoted to extension activities to guide your students to a deeper understanding of the text. It also lets your students know that good readers think about what they read not only while they're reading it, but also after they read. Extension activities can take the form of student-led discussions, written responses, shared writing, drawing, creating alternate endings, and constructing charts and diagrams. It is important that whatever extension activity you choose is designed to help the students extend their knowledge without losing sight of the original text. Homework on this last day consists of each student reading a text of their own choosing. Depending on the number of times the students have read the text at home, each of your students will have read your target text from four to seven times over the course of the week.

Wide Fluency-Oriented Reading Instruction

Wide FORI differs from FORI in that your students read three texts over the 5-day period as opposed to reading and rereading a single text. However, there are several similarities between the two procedures as well. For example, both FORI and Wide FORI have an easy-to-implement, 5-day lesson plan that can be an effective shared reading component of your overall literacy curriculum. Both programs require your students spend 20–30 minutes reading connected text each day and both maintain an emphasis on comprehension. Further, each program uses challenging material to expose students to a variety of concepts, vocabulary, and ideas that would not be accessible if students were limited to instructional-level texts. And, as students encounter these ideas and phrases again—either in new texts or through repetition—they lead to better fluency and improved comprehension (Logan, 1997). Additionally, both strategies provide extensive scaffolding while texts are being read and both incorporate some level of repeated reading, which has been shown to improve fluency and comprehension. And, finally, research has documented the value of both programs.

Wide FORI in Action

Day 1: Introducing the Text

Day 1 of Wide FORI parallels the first day of the FORI procedure in that you begin by introducing the week's text with the same kind of prereading activities that you would normally use. These activities could include introducing vocabulary, building background knowledge, and making predictions about the text and should also help to build interest and promote motivation for reading.

WIDE FORI IN ACTION: WEEKLY LESSON PLAN

	Monday	Tuesday	Wednesday	Thursday	Friday
Wide FORI daily classroom plans	• Teacher introduces the selection to the class using prereading activities. • Teacher reads the selection to the class while the class follows in their individual copies. • Teacher leads discussion of the selection to keep the focus on comprehension.	• Teacher and students echo-read the first selection. • Comprehension strategies should be infused throughout the selection (student questioning, vocabulary work, etc.). • If time permits, students can partner-read the text.	• Students complete extension activities to broaden comprehension of text. • Activities may include student-led discussions, written responses, construction of charts and diagrams, etc.	• Teacher and students echo-read a second selection. • Comprehension remains a focus through activities such as vocabulary work, questioning, and summarizing. • If time permits, students can partner-read the text.	• Teacher and students echo-read a third selection. • Comprehension remains a focus through activities such as vocabulary work, questioning, and summarizing. • If time permits, students can partner-read the text.
Home reading	• Students read a book of their own choosing for 20–30 minutes.	• Students take home target selection and read it to a friend or family member.	• Students who need more practice read the target selection; others read a selection of their own choosing.	• Students read a book of their own choosing for 20–30 minutes.	• Students read a book of their own choosing for 20–30 minutes.

Next, you read the text aloud to the students as they follow along in their own copies. This allows them to hear an expressive, fluent reading of the text without having to decode independently. You will want to circulate around the room as you are reading to monitor which students are following along and which you may need to redirect. Finally, to keep your students focused on comprehension, the reading should be followed by a discussion about some aspect of the book (plot, character, setting) or by a response to the text (writing, drawing). Students should read a book of their own choosing for homework.

Day 2: Echo Reading

The second day of the Wide FORI procedure is again much like Day 2 of the FORI procedure in that you will conduct an echo reading of the primary text. Depending on how much experience your students have with echo reading, you will either begin with reading just a sentence or two to your students and having them echo it back or with longer amounts of text (perhaps a paragraph or two). Eventually, your students may be able to echo-read an entire page depending on the layout of the text. It is also important that you model comprehension strategies within and following the echo reading in order to keep a focus on comprehension. Strategies such as asking your students a range of questions, student-led questioning, and summarization would all be appropriate here. If time permits, the students can partner-read the text after the echo-reading and comprehension activities are through. For homework students should take home their copies of the text and read it aloud to a family member or friend.

Day 3: Extension Activities

Day 3 of the Wide FORI approach is different from FORI in that you do not do another rereading of the primary text. Instead, Day 3 is dedicated to extension activities, such as student-led discussions, written responses, or the use of graphic organizers that help students develop a deeper understanding of the text. Since the students are spending less time on the primary text than in FORI, these extension activities are particularly important for strengthening student comprehension and understanding.

Homework on Day 3 depends on the needs of your students. Students who are fairly comfortable with reading the passage can be given the option of reading something of their own choosing for homework. Students who are still in need of practice on the primary text should read it at home to a family member or friend for a final time.

Days 4 and 5: Echo Reading

Days 4 and 5 are devoted to echo reading and discussing a second and third text, respectively. Since you are only working with each of these texts for 1 day, it is important that you work on developing a solid understanding of what is being read with your students. This can be done through a range of comprehension activities such as vocabulary work, questioning, or summarizing. If time permits, the students can reread the selection with a partner. For homework on each of these days, the students should read that day's selection aloud to a family member or friend.

Finding Appropriate Texts

To use the Wide FORI approach, you will need three classroom sets of texts over the course of each week. Gathering enough materials for your whole class may require you to be a little creative. If your class is using a commercial core program or literature anthology, your primary selection can come from there. If your school is using a guided reading program, you may be able to find enough trade books to create a class set by working with your grade-level colleagues as well as your school library. For instance, if each of four second-grade classrooms might have five or six copies of a book and the library might have an additional one or two. There may also be old editions of core programs available in the store room to use as a second or third text for the week. Student magazines such as *Weekly Reader, Spider Magazine*, and *National Geographic Kids* also have articles that are not only long enough to provide connected text for this activity but deal with important topics as well. Appropriate text can also be downloaded from the Internet and copied for your students (e.g., *kids.usa.gov* provides a myriad of resources). And while the three texts do not need to be conceptually related, when they are, it is likely that the concepts and overlapping vocabulary will be strengthened even further (Adams, 2010–2011; Kuhn et al., 2010; Logan, 1997).

FORI or Wide FORI: Which to Choose?

In a study that looked at both FORI and Wide FORI procedures (Kuhn et al., 2006), students using both approaches made significantly more growth on standardized measures of comprehension and word recognition in isolation than did students in a control group. Importantly, students from both groups still outperformed their peers in comprehension a year later. The students in the Wide FORI group also did better than their peers in both the FORI and control groups on a measure of CWPM, a common measure of automaticity. Although both FORI and Wide FORI are effective fluency approaches, we recommend the use of Wide FORI when possible since the use of multiple texts will afford your students access to a broader range of vocabulary and concepts each week than with a single text. As previously discussed, seeing a word in several different contexts may help a student learn to read the word more easily (Mostow & Beck, 2005). So it may be that Wide FORI benefits students by providing the repetition of words and phrases across a range of contexts. In addition, Wide FORI's use of multiple scaffolded texts may help to lessen the gap in vocabulary and concept knowledge that develops as proficient and nonproficient readers move through the grades (Hirsch, 2003; Stanovich, 1986). However, by providing scaffolded practice with challenging texts, both approaches offer access to vocabulary and concepts for struggling readers that is usually only available to proficient readers. And by helping all students read at a higher level, FORI and Wide FORI lay the groundwork for independent reading success in later grades.

Conclusion

The research base for FORI and Wide FORI shows that they can be effective and easy-to-implement approaches. The most critical features for implementing either approach are the time that your students spend reading connected text—it must be 20 minutes or more daily—and the attention you pay to their implementation. Since you will be using challenging texts, it is also essential that extensive scaffolding take place with the reading that you and your students undertake. It is important that the texts used be at grade level or higher. Research shows that when the texts were not challenging enough the students did not make significant progress. However, even with scaffolding, students should not be given text that is completely beyond their reading ability. Stahl and Heubach (2005) suggest that students can benefit from text that they can read with an accuracy rate of 85% if accompanied by strong support. It is unlikely that anything more difficult than that will be beneficial even with the scaffolding.

Finally, fluency-oriented instruction is not for all students. Emergent readers and those unable to read at the primer level will probably not benefit from this instruction. Alternatively, children who are already fluent readers would be better off working with more challenging fiction and content-area texts. However, these approaches can help to make a substantial contribution to the reading development of those students who have established basic decoding skills but who still are disfluent readers.

CHAPTER 6
. . . .

Fluency Instruction for Flexible Groups

GUIDING QUESTIONS

- Why and how can you use flexible groups to ensure that all your students become fluent readers?
- What specific approaches have researchers tested?
- Why do all of these approaches use challenging texts?
- What role does scaffolding play in the success of these approaches?
- When—and why—should you consider removing this instruction from your curriculum?

Stephanie is a second-grade teacher with a pretty high-flying bunch this year. She was given many of the strong readers coming out of last year's first grade, and the majority of her class is already reading with appropriate fluency and expression. However, there are four or five students who are not making the transition to fluent reading quite as quickly as the others. Last year, when Stephanie had primarily lower-achieving learners, it made sense to spend whole-group time on fluency work, but this year it feels like a disservice to the other kids to spend valuable instructional time on something they are already succeeding at doing. Now what?

Why Flexible Groups for Teaching Fluency?

Most students make the transition to fluent reading between second and third grade so whole-class fluency interventions are most appropriate during those grades. However, some second graders have already reached an acceptable level of fluency and some older students are still not fluent readers. Consequently, whole-class fluency approaches are not always the best use of classroom time. When you are working in a situation where some of your students need fluency instruction but that group is not in the majority, flexible grouping may be the best way to meet the varied needs of your learners.

Flexible groups are fluid groups whose membership is temporary and based on student need or student interest (Reutzel, 2003). Because they are temporary, flexible groups allow you to bring together students for work in a particular area or on a particular skill. The instruction is designed to meet the needs or interests of those specific students; once you have accomplished your goals for the group, you can rework your classroom dynamics to take on another form of instruction.

One option is to use the Wide FORI or FORI lesson plans with smaller groups of students who need extra support becoming fluent readers (Kuhn et al., 2006; see Chapter 5). Another option is to use the approaches presented in this chapter. These approaches were specifically designed for work with small groups of learners and can play a more flexible role in your literacy curriculum. Rasinski's four principles of fluency instruction (Rasinski, 1989)—support, modeling, focus on phrasing, and opportunities for practice—are all critical components of these approaches. The use of challenging text is also an important feature of these practices. All of these factors will assist you in making fluency instruction for flexible groups a beneficial practice within your literacy curriculum, helping to ensure that all of your students develop reading fluency.

Oral Recitation Lesson

In the 1980s Jim Hoffman (1987) and Susan Crone's (Hoffman & Crone, 1985) research sought to find alternatives to round-robin reading as a means of making the basal readers of the time more effective tools for classroom learning. They researched the oral reading practices of the 1800s and found two models of instruction that informed their work. These methods were the recitation lesson and the story method, both of which were successful at developing expressive reading and increasing comprehension. From this research, they designed the Oral Recitation Lesson (ORL) based on the principles used in these older instructional models.

The ORL was originally developed for use with small groups of second graders who were experiencing difficulty with the material in their grade-level readers. The authors explained that there were three fundamental principles that led to the success of the model: comprehension, modeling, and repetition. Comprehension was to be addressed early in the lesson to emphasize its dominant role in reading. Young students, who often thought of reading as pronouncing the words correctly, needed to understand that reading was actually about constructing meaning from text. Word identification was only important as the means for understanding the ideas in a selection. Modeling by the teacher provided the students with a fluent and expressive interpretation of the text. They could hear the text as it was being read aloud and develop an understanding of the concepts presented before being required to decode. Finally, repetition was used to scaffold the learners' reading as they became more comfortable with the text.

The approach was originally designed for use with the narrative selections found in the basal readers of the time, but it can be used with a variety of materials as long as they are challenging to your students. Trade books, commercial core program selections, content-area textbook selections, student magazines, and sources from the Internet would all be appropriate for use here although we find speeches or poems of substantial length readily lend themselves to this instructional approach. ORL incorporates five components in two different phases occurring over several days or a week (see Figure 6.1). The length of the procedure is dependent on the length and complexity of the selection used. The first phase, the direct instruction phase, incorporates a comprehension component, a practice component, and a performance component. The indirect instruction phase includes practice-to-mastery for all of the students. Although the procedure was originally designed for use with struggling second-grade readers, it is effective with any children having trouble making the transition to fluent reading.

The first component of the direct instruction phase begins with you reading the selection to your students in a way that models appropriate expression, pacing, and phrasing. As you are reading, your students should be following along in their own copies of the text. You can monitor their attention to the task by walking around the room as you read. In the original model, the group then constructed a story map with the teacher as the scribe. In this way, the teacher supported students' identification of the title, characters, setting, problem, events, and solution as a precursor to writing a story summary. This story map/summary activity could be replaced by any comprehension activity that will help your students'

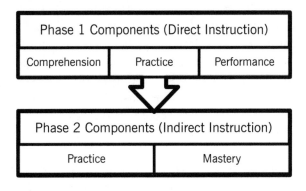

FIGURE 6.1. The two phases of the ORL.

understanding of the text. For example, you could do vocabulary work, explore character development, or discuss alternate endings.

The second component of the direct instruction phase can include a variety of fluency strategies. You can use either echo or choral reading at this point. Which one you choose should depend on the needs of your students; as you know now, echo reading provides greater scaffolding than choral reading. Chapter 4 details the steps for both procedures. This component emphasizes prosodic reading and allows you to move your students away from word-by-word reading toward automatic word recognition, expression, and phrasing.

In the final component of the first phase, students select a section of the text and individually practice their portion with the goal of performing it for their peers. Each student picks a portion no longer than a page. By practicing independently they are able to create their own interpretation of the text. When they are comfortable with the text, they can choose to read it to their classmates. Classroom peers are invited to provide positive feedback. You may want to model what positive feedback looks and sounds like so that your students understand how to respond appropriately to their friends. It is also critical to remember that no child should ever be forced to read aloud. As students see their friends perform, however, they will likely become more motivated to try themselves.

The second phase of the intervention was added when the authors noticed that the struggling readers they were working with needed additional practice to master the passage. This phase can be accomplished during any independent reading time; it can be planned time that you provide for your students or it can occur during "down times" in your instructional day (before morning lessons get under way, in the time before lunch or recess, etc.). You only need to find 10 minutes per day. During this time, students work independently with passages that you have already introduced to the group as part of the direct instruction phase. Students practice reading their passages in a soft whisper, known as "mumble reading," until they feel ready to have you listen to them to check for mastery. *Mastery* is defined as 98% word accuracy, a reading rate that is average for the student's grade level, and reading with appropriate pacing and expression. Once a student has achieved mastery for one section, she or he can move onto practicing for mastery for the next section, depending on the length of the material and the amount of time you want to dedicate to each selection. While the students are all working on the same selection during the direct instruction phase, they may be working on different passages during the indirect instruction phase, depending on how quickly they reach mastery and move on from one section to the next. Students should also be encouraged to take home copies of the selection to read to family and friends for extra practice.

The ORL has helped students to increase both fluency and comprehension (Reutzel & Hollingsworth, 1993; Reutzel, Hollingsworth, & Eldridge, 1994). As such, it can serve as a simple and efficient way to work with flexible groups.

Fluency-Oriented Oral Reading
and Wide Fluency-Oriented Oral Reading

As part of her dissertation, Melanie designed and tested two different fluency approaches to examine the differences between repeated reading and scaffolded wide reading in a small-group setting (Kuhn, 2004–2005). These approaches, known as Fluency-Oriented Oral Reading (FOOR) and Wide Fluency-Oriented Oral Reading (Wide FOOR), are appropriate for small groups of students who are making the transition to fluent reading. The original intervention included struggling second-grade readers using texts ranging from late-first-grade to early-third-grade levels according to Fountas and Pinnell's (1999) ratings. Titles such as *The Fire Cat* (Averill, 1988), *The Case of the Dumb Bells* (Bonsall, 1982), and *Whistle for Willie* (Keats, 1964) were included in the study. Since the instruction was heavily scaffolded, such challenging books could be appropriately used. The groups in the study consisted of five or six students, but you could use this intervention with fewer students and could even use it in a one-to-one tutorial format.

In the original study, the groups of students met three times a week for 15–20 minutes. The FOOR group used a modified repeated reading procedure where the students echo- or choral-read a single title three times over the course of a week. In contrast, the Wide FOOR group echo- or choral-read three different titles during their three weekly meetings. A third group listened to a fluent and expressive reading of the Wide FOOR titles, and a fourth group made up of students from all the classrooms did not receive any additional reading instruction beyond that already taking place in their literacy curriculum.

The study yielded interesting results that can be used to inform your own small-group instruction. Both the FOOR and Wide FOOR groups scored better than the other two groups in the areas of word recognition in isolation, prosody, and correct words read per minute. Additionally, the Wide FOOR group made greater gains than any of the other groups in the area of comprehension. This noteworthy outcome may be due to the type of tasks required by the two different approaches under study. Since there had been no specific comprehension instruction included in any of the sessions, the students in the study may have developed their own sense of what to focus on during the sessions. Since repetition was used during the FOOR intervention, the students might have interpreted the goal of the rereading as improving word recognition and prosody; in other words, they might have thought they were reading it repeatedly until they got it to sound just so. By contrast, the students in the Wide FOOR group may have inferred that they were reading multiple texts because the various stories mattered, and therefore put more emphasis on comprehension. Similar results had been found in earlier repeated reading studies (O'Shea, Sindelar, & O'Shea, 1985, 1987). It seems that merely asking students to focus on the meaning of a text results in increased comprehension. In hindsight, adding a meaning focus to a lesson could have resulted in the

FOOR group making the comprehension gains that the Wide FOOR group made. As such, we suggest you integrate a *brief* comprehension component as part of your lessons when using these approaches.

An essential consideration when implementing either of these strategies is that your students be given the opportunity to work with challenging text over a significant amount of time (15–20 minutes per session). In order to continually challenge your students with the level of text presented, you'll need to reevaluate how well they are reading at a particular text level every few weeks. As they show progress, you will want to keep moving them to the next level of challenge. This continual reevaluation will also let you know when your students have reached the point where grade-level material is at their instructional reading level. When that occurs, you will need to make a decision about whether you still need a fluency component for these students or whether precious instructional time would be better used on comprehension instruction. This may be a tricky decision. Even if they have become fairly fluent with grade-level material, you may want to continue with this work to solidify their reading fluency. However, with some groups, it may be more beneficial to decrease or eliminate the time you work on fluency instruction. Your decision will depend on the specific needs of the group you are working with in a particular school year.

FOOR in Action

Day 1: Introducing the Text

You may start off by *briefly* discussing what the story may be about by using the title and front cover as clues. Your comprehension work should be brief and embedded in your reading of the text since you have limited time and your focus is on fluency. Lead the students in an echo reading of the text. As your students' word recognition improves and they become more comfortable with a given reading level, you can occasionally switch to choral reading for this initial reading.

As you go through the selection, you want to stop intermittently and encourage your students to make inferences or predictions. These occasional pauses in the reading can also be used to clarify aspects of the story or discuss new and interesting words.

Day 2: Partner Reading

On the second day, have your students partner-read the selection. (See Chapter 4 for ways to create partnerships.) Students should work in pairs and read every other page. Since there will be a maximum of three pairs in your group, you will be able to move about the groups and assist students who are having any difficulties.

In the event of an uneven group of students or in the case of an absence, you can act as a reading partner for one of your students; if you always have an uneven

THE 3 DAYS OF FOOR INSTRUCTION

Monday (around 20 minutes)	Wednesday (around 20 minutes)	Friday (around 20 minutes)
• Echo-read the week's text for the first time. • Discuss the selection after you have completed the echo reading.	• Students partner-read the selection. • Depending on time, if the students finish early, they should begin a second partner reading (reading opposite pages from their original reading), even if they aren't able to complete it.	• Choral-read the material for a final time. (If the students need additional support, you can echo-read instead.) • After the final reading, students can practice a section of text and volunteer to read aloud, you can undertake an evaluation of students' fluency, or they can read the material again as partners or individuals.

number of students, you can rotate partners, which should provide an even greater level of support. And if there is enough time after the partners finish the first reading, they can switch pages and reread the text one more time.

Day 3: Choral Reading

On Day 3, you should lead the students in a choral reading of the text. At this point your students should be fairly successful with the text. If, however, your students need more support than the choral reading provides, you can echo-read the text once more. After completing the last reading, students should practice a section of the text. They can then volunteer to read their selection aloud. Alternatively, you can complete a running record or other fluency check (e.g., determining their rate and prosody) of your students' reading to determine how they are progressing or allow them to undertake an additional partner reading or an independent mumble reading of the selection. As long as they spend their time engaged in one of these activities, you should see improvements in their reading fluency. However, it is important to increase the level of text difficulty until the students are fluently reading grade-level material.

Wide FOOR in Action

Day 1: Introducing Text 1

Just as in Day 1 of FOOR, you should introduce the text by *briefly* discussing what it may be about using the title and the cover to provide clues, and then lead the group in an echo reading of the selection. As your students become more proficient readers, you may want to occasionally choral-read on the first day. That

THE 3 DAYS OF WIDE FOOR INSTRUCTION

Monday (around 20 minutes)	Wednesday (around 20 minutes)	Friday (around 20 minutes)
• Echo-read the first text. • Briefly discuss the material as part of the lesson.	• Echo-read the second text. • Briefly discuss the material as part of the lesson.	• Echo-read the third text. • Briefly discuss the material as part of the lesson.

is a decision you can make based on the group's progress over time. However, as students become more skilled with a particular text difficulty level, you should also consider increasing the challenge level of the texts until the students are comfortably reading grade-level material. At this point, you may decide to rethink the focus of this flexible group or decide to rework your groups altogether. As you echo- (or choral-) read, pause occasionally so that students can make predictions based on what they have read so far, clarify vocabulary, or work on comprehension. You can also discuss the selection as a whole at the end of the reading.

Day 2: Introducing Text 2

The second day of the Wide FOOR looks just like the first but with a new text. While the books can be on the same subject (e.g., weather) or incorporate the same theme (e.g., discovery), this is not a requirement. However, it is likely that interlinking texts will serve to further strengthen vocabulary and conceptual knowledge (e.g., Adams, 2010–2011; Kuhn et al., 2010), critical aspects of the CCSS.

Day 3: Introducing Text 3

The third day of Wide FOOR is a repeat of the first two with yet another new selection. The materials used on each of these days could include sets of books from a guided reading program, selections from a commercial core program, trade books, student magazines, or online material. The critical elements to keep in mind are that the material used should always be challenging for the students and that all students must always have their own copies to read from.

Supported Oral Reading

In 1992, Darrell Morris and Laurie Nelson published a study in which they worked with a second-grade teacher in a large urban school district to design a small-group intervention to address the needs of her struggling readers (Morris &

Nelson, 1992). These second graders were working in a grade-level commercial program as the basis of their round-robin reading sessions, but were not experiencing success. Because of the difficulties the students were experiencing, they were beginning to give up on reading altogether. To help these readers, the authors designed a small-group intervention that gave them instructional support in addition to their already-scheduled reading groups.

Morris and Nelson initially designed Supported Oral Reading to be a 2-day approach where the teacher led an echo-reading session on the first day followed by the students reading aloud individually on the second day. However, this 2-day strategy was just not supportive enough for these struggling readers, so the authors redesigned it to increase the number of sessions to three times a week. This gave the students extra scaffolded practice, which helped them make gains over the school year. According to Morris and Nelson, the students improved in the areas of rate, accuracy, and overall reading levels. All of the students made gains on measures of word recognition and eight out of 10 of the students made gains on the Diagnostic Reading Scales (Spache, 1981). In addition, these students, who at the beginning of the year were reading below the preprimer level, attained grade-equivalent scores between 1.5 and 2.2 on the Iowa Test of Basic Skills (ITBS) at the end of the year. They had obviously made some solid gains over the course of the year.

The 3-day Supported Oral Reading procedure can be easily integrated into the flexible grouping component of your literacy program. An every-other-day schedule (Monday–Wednesday–Friday) would work well and give your struggling students important additional support. Morris and Nelson felt that 3 days are necessary for students to develop enough comfort with a given text to feel successful with it prior to moving on to another one. As with other approaches discussed in this book, we encourage you to use challenging texts, but remember what is challenging is defined by the skills of your particular students. In the initial study, the students were reading at the preprimer level, so reading primer or late-first-grade texts would have been challenging.

Each student will need a personal copy of the text, but since you'll be working with small groups, you can look outside your commercial core program or the shared reading texts you use for whole-group instruction in order to find material for this small-group procedure. Further, by choosing from additional sources, you are guaranteeing that your struggling readers are working with at least two different selections per week, one for their primary literacy instruction and one for their Supported Oral Reading lesson. This use of multiple texts will provide your most fragile readers with access to a broader range of vocabulary and concepts than would be the case if you just exposed them to a single text each week. It is important to continually present text that is challenging for them. Otherwise, you may end up presenting selections at your students' independent reading level and further gains will be minimal.

If your students do not seem to be making adequate progress implementing the procedure as outlined, consider adding an additional session prior to Day 2's partner reading; during this time you should echo- or choral-read the text one more time to give the students extra supported practice. Finally, the positive attitude that the study's students developed toward their sessions—and to reading in general—is what you want to foster in your students as well!

Supported Oral Reading in Action

Day 1: Model and Echo Reading

The first day of the Supported Oral Reading procedure begins with you modeling a fluent and expressive reading of the week's selection while your students read along in their own copies. A follow-up discussion of the reading will help your students develop comprehension of the text. After completing the discussion, you should lead the students in either echo reading or mumble reading the text. In this way, you ensure that the students read the texts in a supported manner before having to read it independently.

Day 2: Partner Reading and Independent Practice

On the second day, begin with the students partner reading the text; they should read alternate pages to each other. After the partner reading is complete, have each student select and practice a 100-word passage from the story. They can practice by mumble reading or whisper reading into "phones" that direct the students' voices back to themselves. These "phones" can be made out of PVC pipes or purchased at an educational supply store. If there is enough time, students can finish

---

SUPPORTED ORAL READING LESSON PLAN

Monday (around 20 minutes)	Wednesday (around 20 minutes)	Friday (around 20 minutes)
• Model fluent reading by reading aloud to your group. • Students follow along in their own copies. • Discuss the story and then echo- or mumble-read the selection with the group.	• Students partner-read the text. • They then practice a 100-word passage. • If time allows, they can echo-read the text a second time (reading opposite pages from their original reading).	• Take a running record of the students' reading or evaluate their rate and prosody on the passages they practiced. • Have students who need additional practice read the selection for homework. • Students who are fluent can begin reading a selection of their own choice instead.

the second session by getting back into their pairs for another partner reading of the selection. During this reading, the partners switch places and read the opposite pages from those read initially.

Day 3: Performance and Running Record

On the third day have individual students come up and read to you from the 100-word passage they've been practicing. You can use this opportunity to either measure the students' fluency by determining their CWPM and prosody or undertake a running record of their reading. Students who still appear disfluent can be asked to continue practicing the selection for homework. Students who are reading smoothly and expressively can be encouraged to read another selection of their choosing for homework.

Conclusion

Integrating fluency instruction into flexible groups is an efficient and effective way to meet the varying needs of your students as they develop and change throughout the school year. By using a flexible grouping structure, you can vary your curriculum so that oral reading instruction is targeted to those who need it the most.

It is also important to remember that oral reading instruction, while of great benefit to your students, should not be the entirety of your students' literacy curriculum. It is only one element of a full and balanced curriculum. Further, as your students become comfortable with text that is at or even a bit above their grade level, you will want to phase out fluency-oriented reading instruction in favor of additional comprehension instruction, writing activities, or opportunities to expand your students' reading across a variety of different genres.

CHAPTER 7
• • • • • • • • • •
Fluency Instruction for Individuals

GUIDING QUESTIONS

- What is the origin of repeated readings?
- Under what conditions should you use a reading-while-listening approach?
- When might you consider using cross-age reading?

Josie is a junior at the state university. She is an excited and enthusiastic elementary education major who thought that tutoring at the local elementary school would be a good way to gain extra experience before her senior year and student teaching. When she showed up at Mrs. Griffin's second-grade class, she was happy to be put to work in whatever way she could help. Mrs. Griffin asked her to spend time reading with William who is struggling in the area of reading fluency. While Josie knows she's only being asked to sit in a quiet place and give William the opportunity to read with a caring adult by his side, she really feels that there is more she could do to help William during the time that she's in his classroom.

Making the Most of Opportunities to Work with One or Two Students
• •

There will be occasions when you have the opportunity to work with only one or two students at a time. As a classroom teacher, you may be able to carve out time in your day (lunch, recess, after school, or if you have a paraprofessional to oversee the work of your other students) to work with a particular student who is struggling, but it can also happen if you work as a reading specialist and pull only one or two students for instruction at a time. Additionally, this can happen in a private tutoring situation. In any of these situations, working with an individual student or a group of two allows you to target your instruction to the specific needs of your learners more precisely than if you were working with a whole class. As such, you can provide your readers with specific texts to match every reading activity. For example, your student or students should be using independent-level texts for the reading they do on their own, instructional-level texts for activities where you work on decoding and comprehension, and challenging texts for the fluency-oriented instruction you provide.

Working in one-on-one or one-on-two instructional situations, you will certainly want to spend time on word recognition and comprehension strategies. In addition to that instruction, some of your time would be well spent on fluency development. That being said, it is fortunate that a number of fluency-oriented instructional approaches are designed specifically for individual readers or dyads (pairs of readers).

Before introducing fluency approaches for individuals and dyads that include a good deal of repetition, it is important to emphasize the value of simply reading with your student for a portion of your time together. Students who are struggling with reading typically get far fewer opportunities to engage in reading connected text than do their proficient peers (e.g., Allington, 1991). For these students, independent-level books can be perceived as "baby books" because they are at a lower level than the books read by those around them. Books included as part of their classroom work may be too challenging for these students to attempt to read on their own. Therefore, they spend a minimal amount of time in the kind of sustained reading that their proficient peers routinely engage in.

One of the best ways to provide an individual or pair of students with access to connected text, while at the same time building fluency, is to simply read aloud together. Wait! Didn't we say earlier that you shouldn't have students read aloud from an unpracticed text? Didn't we talk about the problems with round-robin reading? We haven't changed our minds. It's just that there are differences between round-robin reading and the reading you'll do in a one-on-one or one-on-two situation (see Figure 7.1). First, when reading with just one or two readers, each of you would be reading approximately one-third to one-half of the text. In a 30-minute period, that means 10 to 15 minutes of reading per person—as opposed to 1 minute of reading during a 30-minute round-robin session. Second, with a maximum of three readers it is far more likely that each reader is attending when another is reading. If attention wanders, you are much more likely to notice and redirect in the very small group. You can also give your student or students a small break by briefly discussing the text before resuming the reading. Third, the unrehearsed reading is not taking place in front of the class but in an encouraging atmosphere where assistance and support are readily available. When this type of supported

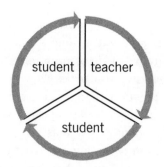

FIGURE 7.1. Shared text reading.

oral reading is done with one or two students, it is critical that each student have his or her own copy of the material being read.

Repeated Readings

Becoming automatic with a skill takes practice. The repeated reading procedure, developed by Jay Samuels (1979), uses that practice to promote a high degree of automaticity with decoding as a means of fostering fluency. Samuels felt that the common educational approach of presenting new material to students each day was not providing students with the amount of practice they needed to develop proficiency. Repeated reading was designed to give students, especially those struggling with the reading task, an opportunity to practice the same material over a number of readings. Samuels asked students to read a short passage several times. As a result, the students' accuracy, speed, and comprehension improved with each successive reading (Figure 7.2). Further, this ability generalized to new texts. That

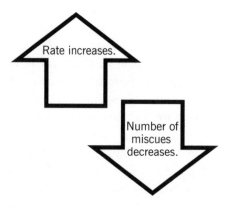

FIGURE 7.2. Results of the repeated readings process.

is, students were able to decode words they practiced in their repeated readings more quickly and efficiently even when they encountered those words in a new selection.

Over the years, there have been numerous studies demonstrating the effectiveness of the repeated reading procedure on measures of accuracy, automaticity, prosody, and comprehension (Dowhower, 1989; Kostewicz & Kubina, 2010). The procedure is easy to implement and very successful when used with an individual reader. Repeated reading is best used with students whose reading is accurate, but slow. These are often word-by-word readers who read at a slow pace even when they come across words that are in their sight-word bank.

The repeated reading procedure takes very little preparation time and can be an especially powerful tool since it allows students to monitor their own progress. As the teacher or tutor, you present the student with a 100- to 200-word passage to read aloud. Keeping the passage at that short length will ensure that the student does not become fatigued when reading it multiple times. The short length will also help you calculate CWPM more easily. Once the student has completed the first "cold" reading of the passage, you calculate the CWPM and the number of miscues and record them on a chart like the one in Figure 7.3. The passage used should have an accuracy rating of between 85 and 90% on the first reading.

Student:		
Title:		
Level:		
	Correct words per minute	**Number of errors**
First reading		
Second reading		
Third reading		
Fourth reading		
Fifth reading		
Criterion:		

FIGURE 7.3. Example of a repeated reading log.

Accuracy ratings outside these limits may prove to be either too challenging or not challenging enough for the student.

The data you collect on that first reading will serve as a baseline against which the student's progress will be compared as he or she rereads the passage. This data tracking can be very motivating for struggling readers who have not previously met with a great deal of reading success (Kuhn & Schwanenflugel, 2006). While data tracking is one of the key features of the repeated reading procedure, we want to caution you not to make reading rate the main focus of the exercise. It is important that students remember that meaning making is the central task of reading. You don't want to create readers who are fast but do not attend to prosody, expression, or comprehension when they read. In order to avoid this, you may want to include a comprehension task in tandem with the texts you use for repeated readings. This can be as simple as telling your students you will be discussing the passage once they have completed their reading. By doing this, you can help make comprehension the centerpiece of your instruction.

In fact, O'Shea, Sindelar, and O'Shea (1985) demonstrated the importance of this idea in their research on repeated readings; they asked the struggling readers who participated either to focus on increasing their reading speed or interpreting the passage's meaning. Both groups increased their reading rate over the course of their readings. However, the students who were asked to focus on meaning also increased their comprehension in comparison to their peers in the other group. Keeping the focus on comprehension can be as simple as asking the student to remember what the passage is about before starting the reading!

It is also important to note limitations regarding the repeated reading procedure. Since the greatest amount of growth occurs between the third and the fifth readings students should keep their repetitions within that range. It is important that you monitor your student to determine whether she or he is reaching the predetermined criterion by the fifth reading. If not, the passages may be too difficult and you might want to consider choosing an easier passage and building up to a more challenging level.

While much previous work has been done to determine target reading rates for students in grades 1–8 (see Table 3.1 in Chapter 3 for an example), you now know that rate is only one characteristic of fluent reading, and an overemphasis on rate to the exclusion of prosody will create fast, but not necessarily fluent, readers. As long as you bear this reality in mind, however, Table 3.1 will help you determine reasonable targets for your students as they work through the repeated reading process.

Once the criterion level has been achieved with one passage, you'll want to assign another passage at the same level of difficulty for your student's next session. You should stay on the same level until the student is able to read a passage at that level with fluency on the first read. Once that happens, you can move the student onto a slightly higher level and continue with the procedure.

In her important review of the repeated reading technique, Dowhower (1989) highlighted a number of its benefits. It promotes faster and more accurate reading, helps struggling readers move from word-by-word reading to the reading of more meaningful phrases, and leads to gains in comprehension (especially when students are encouraged to read for meaning). Additionally, the many studies using a repeated reading procedure since Dowhower's review (e.g., Begeny, Krouse, Ross, & Mitchell, 2009; Musti-Rao, Hawkins, & Barkley, 2009) have confirmed her conclusions.

Repeated Reading in Action

• Choose a 100- to 200-word passage from an appropriately challenging text, one that has a "cold read" accuracy between 85 and 90% correct. Picking a passage of this length will prevent fatigue in your student over the course of several readings.

• Make two copies of the text. One copy will be for the student to use; the second copy will be for you to mark miscues and record the student's rate.

• The student should read the text without any support; you record the number of words the student reads within a minute for this first "cold" reading and mark any miscues he or she might have had. You can let the student continue to read after reaching the minute mark, but only record the number of correct words read in a minute. Transfer the correct words per minute and miscues onto the Repeated Reading Log (Figure 7.3). The accuracy rating on the first reading should be between 85 and 90% to maximize growth.

• Share the results of the initial reading (both correct words per minute and miscues) with the student. Establish a goal for the final rereading. Since the greatest gains for this procedure take place between the third and the fifth reading, we recommend a maximum of five repetitions and an accuracy rate of 98% or better (comparable to an independent reading level). It is important to discuss the goal of the procedure so that the student understands the purpose of rereading the passage and what he or she is trying to accomplish with each successive reading. It is just as important to keep the focus of reading on comprehension, so remind the student that you'll be asking him or her to tell you what the passage is about. This will prevent the student from being overly focused on speed.

• Although not a necessary step of the procedure, you may want to have the student review the passage silently before the second reading. Some children report that this increases their comfort level with the text. The student then rereads the passage a second time and you record the new correct words per minute and number of miscues. The student continues with this procedure, up to five readings. All of the readings do not have to take place in one sitting. Dividing the readings among two or even three sessions gives the student a chance to develop familiarity with the text.

• Set the goal for miscues at one or two per 100 words. If you were to require perfect word reading accuracy (100%), that requirement might slow down your student's reading, which would be counterproductive! Similarly, if your student is missing the same one or two words repeatedly, point out the correct pronunciation of the word after the reading is completed, but don't dwell on it; overemphasizing it can cause the miscue to become a continuing problem for the reader.

• If your student isn't achieving the criteria after five repetitions of the text, you may be choosing texts that are too difficult. Move to an easier passage, one at a lower level. Again, check that the accuracy level is between 85 and 90% on the first read. You may also need to revisit your goal for reaching the criteria for very slow readers. These readers might not be able to make the increases in speed that you first predicted, and you might need to adjust your expectation in increased rate for individual readers.

• When the student has reached the predetermined reading rate and number of miscues on a passage, the next passage should be at the same level of difficulty. This same level should be maintained until the student can do a first "cold read" at that level with fluency. At that point, you can move the student to passages at a slightly higher level of difficulty.

Reading-While-Listening

Reading-while-listening was developed by Carol Chomsky (1976) to assist five third graders who were struggling with reading development. These students were successful at identifying words and using word recognition strategies in isolation, but could not apply that knowledge to connected text. They were all reading 1 or 2 years below grade level and disliked reading. Rather than giving these students more decoding instruction (which wasn't transferring to connected text and was turning them off reading), Chomsky developed a way to expose these students to a significant amount of text in a more accessible format. She selected two dozen books that ranged from second- through fifth-grade reading levels and recorded them. These books were too challenging for the students to read on their own, so Chomsky instructed the students to listen to the recordings repeatedly as they read along with the text. They were allowed to choose from the available tapes, determine their own pace for reading them, and read along with the selections until they could read the material fluently.

Early on, students had some difficulty coordinating their eye movements with the recorded voice. With time and practice, however, it became easier to listen to the reading while simultaneously keeping track of the text. They also stayed with the same selection until they were able to provide a fluent, independent reading of it. At that point, they moved on to the next book and tape. The role of practice on the students' overall fluency development cannot be overemphasized. It took less time to reach mastery (fluent reading) on each subsequent selection. That is, the students were not only improving their word recognition and reading rate, but their gains were transferring to unread selections. In addition, anecdotal evidence from parents and teachers demonstrated that the students were more willing to read independently and to engage in writing activities than they had been before the intervention. Ultimately, the procedure helped students become more engaged readers.

The original reading-while-listening procedure allowed students to independently determine the length and frequency of their sessions. However, you may want to set a timeframe for your student. He or she could read along with a recording of a book during independent reading time or as part of a center since this procedure requires less direct monitoring than a traditional repeated reading procedure. You may be concerned that this activity could turn into a listening activity rather than a reading activity if the student is not actively engaged in the reading, but students will be active participants as long as they are held accountable for their reading. You can do this by completing a fluency assessment at the end of the selection or just by having the student read to you regularly (say once a week). Students enjoy this procedure, and their confidence increases as their success with various texts build.

It is the case that reading-while-listening is more time-consuming than other procedures discussed in this chapter in terms of organization. To decrease the amount of time it takes to prepare recordings for the procedure, you might consider buying unabridged recordings of books. Many are readily available. Alternatively, while this approach was designed for individual learners, Paul Hollingsworth (1978) used recordings with a number of students at once. He used an adapter that allowed several students to listen to the same recording simultaneously. As long as the students are reading along while listening (and being held accountable for that reading) and the pacing and challenge level are appropriate, this modification can help you use the method with a flexible group or in a center with more than one student at a time.

Reading-While-Listening in Action

• Record or purchase the narrated versions of a range of materials for your struggling readers. These should always be the unabridged versions to ensure your students will be able to follow along in the text. You can also recruit volunteers to create recordings, but they must read both smoothly and expressively since they will provide the model for your students' fluent reading. Tape recordings, CDs, and podcasts should all be considered as viable options depending on what type of players you have in the classroom (computers, tablets, tape recorders, etc.).

• Explain to your students that they are not just listening to the story, but should be reading along so they can improve their own reading. At first, students may want to mumble- or whisper-read along with the recording to keep their place. In fact, you may want to provide a "phone" made out of PVC pipes to minimize this noise initially. Encourage students to shift to silent reading as they become more familiar with the procedure. Their goal is to read silently along with the tape.

• When your student is ready to read the text without the support of the recording, have him or her read it to you unassisted. You can listen to the overall reading and assess it using an inventory such as the NAEP Oral Reading Fluency Scale or the Multidimensional Fluency Scale (see pages 35 and 36 in Chapter 3) coupled with a CWPM rating or you may want to use a running record. If you think your student is acceptably fluent, you can have him or her continue the procedure with the next chapter of the same selection or with another selection at the same level. When you feel the level is no longer challenging enough, you can move to a more difficult text (and if he or she hasn't completed the current selection, he or she can do so independently). If fluency is still an issue using the current selection, the student should either continue to practice with it or, if experiencing significant difficulty, move to an easier text.

• It is important to have a variety of materials available. Students should be using material at the top end of their instructional level as well as more difficult text. In Chomsky's (1976) original study, students were reading at the first-through second-grade reading levels, but were using texts ranging from the second- through fifth-grade reading levels. Consider books with short chapters (e.g., *Minnie and Moo and the Potato from Planet X* [Cazet, 2003]) as well as books with longer chapters (e.g., *Aliens Ate My Homework* [Coville, 2007]) and other books that are not broken up into chapters (e.g., *Harry, the Dirty Dog* [Zion, 2006]). In this way you are giving the student the power (and the responsibility) to select the amount of text he or she will be accountable for at any given time. This lets each child work at his or her comfort level.

Cross-Age Reading

One dilemma that teachers of older struggling readers have encountered is getting these students to practice reading repeatedly with books that are appropriate for their reading level. These students don't want to be seen reading books that they consider "babyish." However, books written for younger readers might be at just the right level for older struggling readers. To address this dilemma, Labbo and

Teale (1990) developed the cross-age reading strategy to provide older students with a purpose for practicing with lower-level texts. Originally developed for a group of 20 fifth graders, students were asked to read selected books to kindergartners. To prepare for their performance, the older students read a selection repeatedly, giving them the needed practice to develop a fluent rendering of the text.

The fifth graders prepared for the reading in three ways (see Figure 7.4). First, they selected texts that they thought kindergartners would enjoy. Next, they practiced reading them until their reading was smooth and expressive. Finally, the fifth graders were taught a number of ways to engage with the kindergarten students in a discussion about the book. This last point helped to keep the readers and their audience focused on comprehension.

The original study contained three groups: a cross-age reading group, a group that spent time working with kindergarten students on art activities, and a group that participated in typical reading instruction. The cross-age readers made significant gains in both their use of reading strategies and their self-confidence in the area of reading when compared to either of the other two groups. Both fifth graders and kindergartners also reported enjoying the reading sessions.

Cross-Age Reading in Action

• Help your student select a text that a younger student would enjoy listening to and that would provide some challenge for your older reader. Make sure that

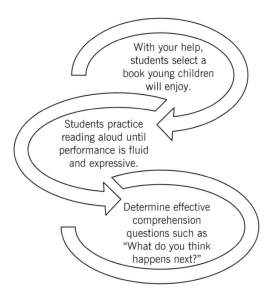

FIGURE 7.4. The three components of a successful cross-age performance.

such books are not so challenging that they negatively affect your older student's motivation. Depending on the current level of your struggling reader, it could be a relatively simple chapter book (e.g., *Henry and Mudge* [Rylant, 1996]) or a more complex picture book (e.g., *Cloudy with a Chance of Meatballs* [Barrett, 1978]).

• Your student should practice reading the text until he or she can read it fluently and with expression. Since this is a book that the student will be practicing on his or her own, it should be closer to his or her independent level than would be the case for most other strategies we've presented that are more heavily scaffolded. The book should be between 90 and 95% accuracy on a first read. As the student continues to practice and read with success, subsequent texts can be increasingly more challenging.

• Demonstrate for your student how he or she should engage the kindergartners he or she will be working with by asking questions that will require the kindergartners to think about the reading. One way to do this is to work with the older reader to identify places in the book where he or she should pause and encourage the kindergartners to make a prediction ("What might happen next?"). Practicing this simple reading strategy may very well transfer to the student's own reading and help him or her better understand higher-level texts.

• It is also worth considering the option of having your students record the stories that they practice. This will make oral copies of the selections available in the primary classroom or the school library's listening center, something that is likely to instill pride and confidence in your older reader while providing a service for your colleagues.

Neurological Impress Method

The neurological impress method (NIM) developed by R. G. Heckelman (1969, 1986), was a staple of the research literature on reading fluency from the 1960s through the 1980s. Heckelman described it as a multisensory approach in which the student sits in front of the teacher while the teacher directs his or her voice into the student's ear as they read in unison. The idea was that the method would "impress" the words on the learner's brain as the teacher spoke directly into his or her ear while the reader tracked the text. This explanation and the implementation of the method appear a bit outdated today; nonetheless, it is an effective strategy. This effectiveness is more likely due to the fact that the teacher is providing the support of unison reading while tracking the text than to the positioning of the teacher's voice to the student's ear, and it seems far more sensible to sit next to the student than behind him or her!

With the provision of such a high level of support, you can pick books to read that your student would not typically be able to handle. This may lead to very motivating choices for your student. Often, struggling readers miss out on the "hot" book or series of the moment because they are unable to successfully read them. This puts them at a disadvantage with their classmates who are all reading a specific popular book. NIM may be a way to expose your struggling reader to a popular, but previously unattainable, text.

As a strategy, NIM has many features that are essential to fluency development. It provides the assistance of a skilled reader as a model, along with practice that is supported by that skilled reader. The student and teacher track the text as it is being read to reinforce the connection between oral and written language and the teacher also emphasizes the prosodic elements of the reading as it is taking place.

While implementing the method, you should vary the pace and volume of the reading. Over the course of the reading you should read faster, slower, softer, or louder as the text dictates. The unison reading should continue until you notice that the student is starting to tire. Since this is such an intense intervention, the student may, at first, only be able to read in this way for 5 minutes. Even with practice, most students won't go beyond 15 minutes. Once your student becomes more capable with a given text level, you can move onto more challenging selections and encourage the student to read material written on the previous level independently. This strategy can be especially effective if you use a series of books such as the *Curious George* books (Rey, 1973; see page 86 for examples of series). The repetition of key words across books will help your student read the texts independently, which will allow you to move onto texts at a higher level for your instructional selections.

NIM in Action

- Select a text that is both motivating and somewhat challenging for your student.

- Sit side by side with your student and have a copy of the text for each of you. It is very important that each of you has your own copy whenever you are reading with, rather than to, a student. In this way, the student can read along at the same time he or she is solidifying his or her knowledge of the speech–print connection and establishing a feeling of ownership over the text.

- Begin unison reading with the student at a moderate rate. You don't want to slow down to match the reader's rate, but rather encourage the reader to increase his pace and match the rhythm of your prosodic reading. If your student is not able to keep up with the pace of your reading, you can slow it down a bit. However, do not slow it down so much that your phrasing becomes awkward and you start reading in a word-by-word fashion. If your student is still not able to keep up with you, you may need to reexamine the text level and move down to a text that is closer to the student's instructional level.

POSSIBLE SERIES BOOKS

A to Z Mysteries by Ron Roy

Amy Hodgepodge by Kim Wayans and Kevin Knotts

Beast Quest by Adam Blade

Beezus and Ramona by Beverly Cleary

Cam Jansen by David Adler

Clubhouse Mysteries by Sharon M. Draper

Commander Toad by Jane Yolen

Curious George by H. A. Rey

Diary of a Wimpy Kid by Jeff Kinney

The Dork Diaries by Rachel Renee Russell

Dragonbreath by Ursula Vernon

Dyamonde Daniel by Nikki Grimes

George and Martha by James Marshall

Geronimo Stilton books (e.g., *Lost Treasures of the Emerald Eye*)

Henry Huggins by Beverly Cleary

Ivy and Bean by Annie Barrows

Judy Moody by Megan McDonald

Keena Ford by Melissa Thomson

Little Bill by Bill Cosby

Mary Pope Osborne books (e.g., *Dinosaurs before Dark*)

My Father's Dragon by Ruth Stiles Gannett

My Weird School by Dan Gutman

Ruby and the Booker Boys by Derrick Barnes

The Sisters Grimm by Michael Buckley

Stink by Megan McDonald

Sugar Plum Ballerinas by Whoppi Goldberg

Time-Warp Trio by Jon Scieszka

Warriors by Erin Hunter

- Vary the reading pace, expression, and volume to help the student gain familiarity with hearing and reading various interpretations of a selection.

- Always be aware if the student is starting to experience fatigue, but try to build stamina by initially reading from the same text for 5 minutes. This heavily scaffolded approach can help struggling students build reading stamina, which will be essential for their later reading success.

- When your student seems to be keeping up with your reading rate while maintaining an expressive rendition of the selection, you may want to "drop back" and allow him or her to take the lead in finishing the section. If he or she stumbles, however, simply slip back into unison reading again.

- Once your student seems comfortable with a given level of text, you should consider moving to a more challenging level to ensure continued progress.

Conclusion

If you are lucky enough to be in a situation where you can work with one or two students at a time, then any of the previously discussed strategies could meet your needs. If, however, your current classroom structure cannot support these very individualized approaches, then you may want to integrate reading-while-listening or cross-age reading into your literacy centers or your independent reading time. By providing these options to all of your readers, not just the ones who are struggling, you can avoid stigmatizing your struggling readers while simultaneously providing them with the support they need.

CHAPTER 8

• • • • • • • • • • •

Supplemental
Fluency Instruction

GUIDING QUESTIONS

• •

- When and why should you use supplemental fluency instruction with your class?
- When should you consider using paired repeated reading in your curriculum?
- When should you consider using the Fluency Development Lesson with your learners?
- How and when can Readers' Theatre supplement your work?

Matt is really pleased with the progress of his second-grade students. As a group, they are making steady growth in decoding and comprehension. Fluency is not a huge concern for the group as a whole, but he realizes that as the texts become more complex his students may, at times, be challenged in the area of fluency. For this reason he has decided to include fluency activities as a supplement to his overall literacy program.

Why Supplemental Fluency Instruction?

Not all of the classes that you teach will struggle with fluency. However, just because your students are making progress doesn't mean they won't benefit from your use of an occasional fluency strategy to ensure their continued development. The methods presented in this chapter can be used to supplement your literacy program to ensure that each student has the opportunity to develop fluency along with other important areas of literacy.

Paired Repeated Reading

· ·

During the 1980s Patricia Koskinen and Irene Blum (1984, 1986) developed a repeated reading technique that maximized the benefits of the original repeated reading procedure while minimizing some of the management challenges it presented. As in the more traditional repeated reading procedure, paired repeated reading helps students to increase automaticity and word recognition, and leads to a more prosodic rendering of the text. However, the original repeated reading technique can be challenging to implement with more than one or two children due to its reliance on teacher feedback and recording changes across readings. Koskinen and Blum designed the repetition to take place in the context of partner reading so that the partners could provide the feedback. In their research, the authors found that there were significant differences between students who used the procedure and those who did not in the areas of oral fluency and comprehension. The below-average third graders in their study also made fewer meaning-changing miscues than their peers.

Paired repeated reading can be used with any text, including core selections, trade books, and content-area texts. It can be used with the entire class during a shared reading period or with a particular group of students while you are working with others. While the focus of the procedure is on increasing rate and accuracy, the use of a listener keeps attention on prosodic elements such as phrasing and expression. This procedure requires a minimum of teacher preparation and typically takes only 10–15 minutes to complete (see Figure 8.1).

Pairs of students pick two 50-word passages from a previously read text to read aloud. To begin, each child in the pair reads to him- or herself. Then one of the pair takes on the role of reader; he or she will read his or her passage aloud to the listener three times in a row. After each reading, the reader self-evaluates the reading. After the second and third readings, the listener also provides positive feedback on the reader's performance. After these three oral readings, the roles are reversed and the repeated readings and feedback takes place again with the students assuming their new roles.

Paired Repeated Reading in Action

• Before you undertake your first session with your students, you'll want to model your expectations for appropriate partner-reading behavior. Since you may have several partners working at once, you will want to start with your expectations for speaker volume. Your students can practice the difference between "inside" and "outside" voices; you may want to be even more specific and model the difference between a whole-group voice and a partner-reading voice.

• Model ways in which your students can provide positive feedback to their partners. Encourage a positive approach in which students coach their partners

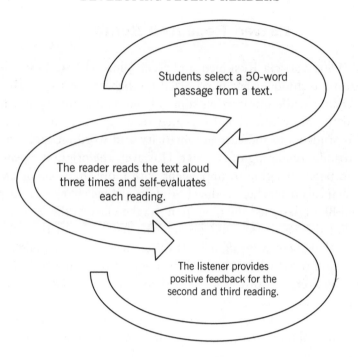

FIGURE 8.1. Steps in the paired repeated readings procedure.

with helpful comments. Comments can include, "You were able to read more quickly this time through" or "You read more of the words correctly than on the last read." It may be helpful to have the class brainstorm a list of positive comments a listener could make and leave the list prominently displayed in your classroom as a reminder and prompt for your students.

• To begin the procedure, complete an initial whole-class reading and discussion of a story, book, or content-area text. Then allow students to form pairs. Students can determine who will be the first reader. Alternatively, you could create a schedule in which students rotate being the first reader as a means of avoiding disagreements.

• Each student selects his or her own passage of approximately 50 words from the material. Partners are encouraged to select different 50-word passages to minimize direct comparisons between the reading performance of the partners.

• Students read through their passages silently.

• The first student reads the passage aloud three times. After each reading, the student evaluates his or her reading by rating it and recording any improvements on a self-evaluation sheet such as the one in Figure 8.2.

- The listening partner listens carefully to the reader and provides positive feedback after the second and third readings. In this way, the listener is commenting on improvement between readings. The listener's comments are recorded on a listener's sheet like the one in Figure 8.3.

- The roles are then reversed and the process is repeated.

Reader's Name: _____

Listener's Name: _____

Date: _____

First reading: How well did you read?

Second reading: How well did you read?

Third reading: How well did you read?

FIGURE 8.2. Reader's Checklist for paired repeated reading.

Reader's Name: _____

Listener's Name: _____

Date: _____

Second reading: How did your partner improve on this reading?

____smoother

____knew more words

____better expression

Other comments: _____

_____

Third reading: How did your partner improve on this reading?

____smoother

____knew more words

____better expression

Other comments: _____

_____

FIGURE 8.3. Listener's Checklist for paired repeated reading.

Fluency Development Lesson

In 1994, Timothy Rasinski and his colleagues published a study designed to evaluate the effectiveness of the Fluency Development Lesson (FDL; Rasinski, Padak, Linek, & Sturtevant, 1994). The FDL was designed as a supplement to the regular reading curriculum and used in the urban second-grade classrooms the researchers studied. Two second-grade classrooms used the FDL as a supplement to the literacy activities they were already using. Another two second-grade classrooms participated in other activities to supplement their literacy curriculum. However, the teachers for these two control classrooms were encouraged to minimize their use of repetition. Students in the FDL classrooms made significant gains in reading rate in comparison to their control-group peers as measured by an informal reading inventory. Noting the importance of automaticity as a component of reading fluency, these results suggest that the FDL can be a useful way to integrate fluency into your overall literacy curriculum.

The FDL was designed to be easily administered. It takes approximately 15 minutes and can be used to supplement a regular reading curriculum. It incorporates Rasinski's principles of effective fluency instruction: modeling, oral support and assistance, practice, and appropriate phrasing (see Chapter 5 for a more detailed explanation of these principles).

The FDL begins with the teacher's fluent reading of a short, usually predictable text of 50–150 words. This can be a passage from a core program, trade book, or content-area text. The original authors found short poems worked very well for this purpose. The passage or poem is read several times to provide a model of fluent reading as well as repetition. The students follow along silently in their own copy of the selection. Then the class participates in a 2- to 3-minute discussion on the meaning of the poem or passage and any difficult or unusual words encountered. Next, the teacher leads the class in several choral readings of the passage. Each choral reading can use a different voice or cadence to help children "play" with the language and experiment with fluency. At this point, the group breaks up into pairs and the procedure follows a similar format to that of paired repeated reading. Finally, the students are brought back together in the large group, and volunteers read the passage or poem for their peers or for classroom guests. Students are given a copy of the text to take home and read to a family member or friend for extra practice.

The FDL is easily incorporated into your current literacy curriculum due to its use of short texts (50–150 words), fast pace, and minimal teacher preparation time. It is an appropriate procedure to use with young children and older struggling readers. When choosing texts for older struggling students, keep in mind that they may be more open to the use of poems, excerpts from speeches, and passages from nonfiction texts. Their motivation will increase if they are comfortable with the kind of text presented. You can also use a short passage taken from a longer text that you have been discussing as part of the shared reading component of your literacy program. Different short passages from a text like this could be used on several consecutive days.

Because of the brevity of the passages presented and the ease in which FDL can be incorporated into your existing curriculum, it is an easy way to have students practice reading both widely and repeatedly.

FDL in Action

• After making sure students have individual copies to follow along in, read a passage or poem aloud several times, modeling appropriate expression and phrasing.

• Lead a short discussion about the text's meaning and call attention to any words that may be particularly interesting or tricky for your students.

- Have your students break into pairs and practice reading the text three times. While the first student is reading, his or her partner is responsible for listening. The listener is also responsible for providing positive feedback to the reader (see the section on paired repeated readings earlier in the chapter for a discussion on how to model positive feedback between partners).

- Students come back together in the large group and volunteers can read aloud to their peers and/or invited classroom guest (principal, parents, etc.).

- Each student takes home a copy of the passage to read again to a parent or friend.

- The following day the passage or poem can be read one more time before a new text is used for the next FDL.

Readers' Theatre

Readers' Theatre is a motivating way to supplement your literacy curriculum. It gives students a purposeful and authentic context for repeatedly reading a text and encourages them to respond to and interpret literature through their expressive rendering of scripts. In Readers' Theatre, students prepare for a performance that does not require costumes, makeup, sets, props, or even the memorization of lines. The performance takes place with scripts in hand as the students make the story, speech, or poem come alive with their voices.

Readers' Theatre is a supplemental activity. Unfortunately, it has taken over some classroom curricula because it is fun and motivating. While it is a great way to supplement what you are already doing in the classroom, it is not a literacy curriculum on its own. However, it is a great way to inject a dose of fun into your literacy period and reinforce the social nature of reading.

Readers' Theatre helps students develop fluency while placing a strong emphasis on the use of appropriate expression and pacing to convey the meaning of a text. It is a flexible approach that can be used with a small group or with your entire class and gives students a reason to practice a selection. When groups of students work on the same passage in a choral reading fashion, the struggling readers will hear the model of skilled readers and the more proficient readers can help others with pronunciation, expression, and pacing. It is also important that struggling readers are given parts of a reasonable length since these students are most in need of practice. In fact, they are unlikely to develop automatic word recognition, pacing, and expression if the part they are given is too small.

Scripts should be age- and grade-level appropriate in content and readability, as well as interesting and inclusive of rich vocabulary. Scripts can be purchased through publishers and book vendors and many are now available online to be downloaded and printed for free! Some of these sites are listed on the next page.

WEBSITES WITH FREE READERS' THEATRE SCRIPTS

www.teachingheart.net/readerstheater.htm

www.aaronshep.com/rt

www.timelessteacherstuff.com

http://storiestogrowby.com/script.html

http://havefunteaching.com/activities/reading/activities/readers-theater

Literature anthologies and basal readers often contain plays or poems for multiple voices. These kinds of texts may also be available in collections in your school or public library.

Alternatively, you could rewrite a text or portion of a text into a play-like format. When writing Readers' Theatre scripts it is useful to have at least one narrator; if the narrated text becomes too lengthy, the narration duties can be split between two or even three narrators. Their role is to describe the action, establish the setting, and "paint a picture" for the listener. You may also find it beneficial to work with another teacher in your building to incorporate older students in the rewriting of a text as a Readers' Theatre script. This gives the older students writing practice with a purpose and helps you to accrue a collection of scripts.

Readers' Theatre in Action

• Select a poem, play, or story that the students will enjoy and that has grade-appropriate content. The text should be somewhat challenging for the majority of your students since they will be spending time reading it repeatedly.

• Since you are going to use a somewhat challenging text, it is important that you read aloud the entire piece to your class before they attempt it on their own. Students read along with their own copies as you present the selection. This first reading gives them visual as well as auditory input. If the text is going to be a particular challenge for the class, you may want to echo- or choral-read it again before assigning parts.

• After your initial whole-class reading is completed, divide the students into groups. You can use Readers' Theatre as a whole-class activity with a single text or use multiple texts and divide your class into smaller, flexible groups. By breaking your class into smaller groups you can match groups and scripts more precisely and give students more substantial parts.

• Make sure that each group's script is sufficiently challenging so that the activity remains an effective aid for fluency development. As an alternative, you could give several students the same role and have them perform it chorally. This gives each individual reader additional support.

• Your students should be given plenty of time to practice their parts. They can practice both individually and in their groups, reading silently and aloud. Group members should be encouraged to give positive feedback to each other as they prepare for their performance.

• Students can perform their script for their classmates or for other classroom guests (e.g., parents, principal, school secretary, or custodian).

Conclusion

The supplemental procedures described above provide well-researched activities that can be incorporated into any literacy program. They can be used when you want to shine a light on fluency or when you are ready to revisit this very important reading component in a fun and motivating way. However, it is important to remember that these are supplemental activities; for a more comprehensive fluency program for either the whole class, a small group, or individuals, the methodologies presented in earlier chapters would be more appropriate.

Recommended Trade Books
for Children by Theme

History

Aunt Harriet's Underground Railroad in the Sky, written by Faith Ringold. Crown Publisher, 1992.

The Courage of Sarah Noble, written by Alice Dalgliesh. Aladdin, 1991.[a]

The Drinking Gourd: A Story of the Underground Railroad, written by F. N. Mongo. Harper-Collins, 1993.

Fifty Cents and a Dream, written by Jabari Asim. Little, Brown Books for Young Readers, 2012.[b]

George Washington's Breakfast, written by Jean Fitz. Houghton Mifflin, 1989.

Henry's Freedom Box: A True Story from the Underground Railroad, written by Ellen Levine. Scholastic, 2007.[c]

If You Grew Up with Abraham Lincoln, written by Ann McGovern. Scholastic, 1992.

If You Grew Up with George Washington, written by Ruth Belov Gross. Scholastic, 1982.

If You Lived in the Time of Martin Luther King, written by Ellen Levine. Scholastic, 1990.

If You Sailed on the Mayflower in 1620, written by Ann McGovern. Scholastic, 1991.

If You Traveled in a Covered Wagon, written by Ellen Levine. Scholastic, 1991.

More Than Anything Else, written by Marie Bradby. Orchard, 1995.

Pink and Say, written by Patricia Polacco. Philomel, 1994.

Sweet Clara and the Freedom Quilt, written by Deborah Hopkinson. Knopf, 1993.

Sea Creatures/Ocean

Dancing with the Manatees, written by Faith McNulty. Scholastic, 1994.

A Day Under Water, written by Deborah Kovacs. Scholastic, 1987.

Discovering Whales and Dolphins, written by Janet Craig. Troll, 1990.

Dolphin, written by Robert A. Morris. HarperCollins, 1983.

---

[a]A Newbery Honor Book; [b]Carter G. Woodson Book Award; [c]Caldecott Honor Book; [d]Outstanding Science Trade Books for Children; [e]Pura Belpre Narrative Award; [f]Caldecott Medal Winner; [g]Association of Jewish Libraries Award; [h]Sibert Medal Honor Book; [i]Coretta Scott King Honor Book.

Exploring an Ocean Tide Pool, written by Jean Bendick. Henry Holt and Company, 1994.
Follow the Water from Brook to Ocean, written by Arthur Dorros. HarperCollins, 1991.
Giant Pacific Octopus, written by Leon Gray. Bearport Publishing, 2013.
Going on a Whale Watch, written by Bruce McMillan. Scholastic, 1992.
Here Comes the Humpbacks!, written by April Pulley Sayre. Charlesbridge, 2013.[d]
Hungry, Hungry Sharks, written by Joanna Cole. Random House, 1986.
My Visit to the Aquarium, written by Aliki. HarperCollins, 1993.
Playing with Penguins and Other Adventures in Antarctica, written by Ann McGovern. Scholastic, 1994.
Sea Turtles, written by Caroline Arnold. Scholastic, 1994.
See the Ocean, written by Estella Condra. Ideals Children's Books, 1994.[d]
Under the Sea from A to Z, written by Anne Doubilet. Scholastic, 1991.
Whales, written by Kevin Holmes. Bridgestone, 1998.

Habitats

The Desert beneath the Sea, written by Ann McGovern and Eugenie Clark. Scholastic, 1991.
Desert Giant: The World of the Saguaro Cactus, written by Barbara Bash. Little, Brown, 1989.
The Desert Is Theirs, written by Byrd Baylor. Aladdin, 1975.
Flashy Fantastic Rain Forest Frogs, written by Dorothy Hinshaw Patent. Scholastic, 1997.
The Great Kapok Tree, written by Lynn Cherry. Trumpet Club, 1990.
Life in the Deserts, written by Lucy Baker. Scholastic, 1990.
Life in the Mountains, written by Catherine Bradley. Scholastic, 1991.
Life in the Rain Forests, written by Lucy Baker. Scholastic, 1990.
A Tale of Antarctica, written by Ulco Glimmerveen. Scholastic, 1989.

Dinosaurs

Digging Up Dinosaurs, written by Aliki. HarperCollins, 1988.
Dinosaurs, written by Gail Gibbons. Scholastic, 1987.
Dinosaur Bones, written by Aliki. HarperCollins, 1988.
Dinosaurs are Different, written by Aliki. HarperCollins, 1985.
Dinosaurs and More Dinosaurs, written by M. Jean Craig. Scholastic, 1982.
The Dinosaur who Lived in My Backyard, written by B. G. Hennessy. Puffin, 1990.
Dinosaur Story written by Joanna Cole. Scholastic, 1983.
Giant Dinosaurs, written by Peter Dodson and Peter Lerangis. Scholastic, 1990.
Hunting the Dinosaurs and Other Prehistoric Animals, written by Dougal Dixon. Scholastic, 1987.
My Visit to the Dinosaurs, written by Aliki. HarperCollins, 1985.
Patrick's Dinosaurs, written by Carol Carrick. Clarion Books, 1983.
Tracking Tyrannosaurs, written by Christopher Sloan. National Geographic Society, 2013.

Weather

The Cloud Book, written by Tomie de Paola. Scholastic, 1975.
Clouds, Rain, and Fog, written by Fred and Jeanne Biddulph. Wright Group, 1993.

Cloudy with a Chance of Meatballs, written by Judi Barrett. Aladdin, 1978.

Hurricanes! written by Lorraine Jean Hopping. Scholastic, 1994.

The Living, written by Matt de la Pena. Delacorte Press. 2013.[e]

National Geographic Kids Everything Weather: Facts, Photos, and Fun That Will Blow You Away, written by Kathy Furgang. National Geographic Children's Books, 2012.

The Snowy Day, written by Ezra Jack Keats. Puffin. 1976.

Tornadoes! written by Lorraine Jean Hopping. Scholastic, 1994.

Weather, written by Seymour Simon. HarperCollins, 2006.

Friendship

Amos and Boris, written by William Steig. Scholastic, 1971.

The Family under the Bridge, written by Natalie Savage Carlson. Scholastic, 1990.[a]

The Hundred Dresses, written by Eleanor Estes. HMH Books for Young Children, 2004.[a]

Kermit the Hermit, written by Bill Peet. Houghton Mifflin, 1993.

Mirette on the High Wire, written by Emily Arnold McCully. Scholastic, 1992.[f]

The One and Only Ivan, written by Katherine Applegate. HarperCollins, 2012.

One Cool Friend, written by Toni Buzzeo. Dial, 2012.[c]

The Snail and the Whale, written by Julia Donaldson. Puffin, 2006.

Family

26 Fairmont Avenue, written by Tomie de Paola. Puffin, 1999.

A Chair for My Mother, written by Vera B. Williams. Scholastic, 1982.[c]

Just Me and Mom, written by Mercer Mayer. Random House Books for Young Readers, 2001.

The Keeping Quilt, written by Patricia Polacco. Aladdin, 1998.[g]

The Memory Box, written by Mary Bahr. Whitman, 1992.

My Rotten Redheaded Older Brother, written by Patricia Polacco. Aladdin, 1998.

Nana Upstairs, Nana Downstairs, written by Tomie de Paola. Puffin, 2000.

The Oxcart Man, written by Donald Hall. Puffin, 1979.

The Rag Coat, written by Lauren Mills. Little, Brown, 1991.

The Relatives Came, written by Cynthia Rylant. Scholastic, 1993.[c]

Fables/Fairy Tales/Folk Tales

Extra Yarn, written by Mac Barnett. Balzer & Bray, 2012.[c]

The Eye of the Needle, retold by Teri Sloat. Puffin, 1990.

Fables, written by Arnold Lobel. HarperCollins, 1980.[f]

How Many Spots Does a Leopard Have?: And Other Folktales, written by Julius Lester. Scholastic, 1989.

Johnny Appleseed, retold by Steven Kellogg. Scholastic, 1988.

Mike Fink, written by Steven Kellogg. Scholastic, 1992.

The Mitten, adapted by Jan Brett. Scholastic, 1989.

Paul Bunyan, written by Steven Kellogg. Scholastic, 1984.

Pecos Bill, written by Steven Kellogg. Scholastic, 1992.

Peter and the Wind, retold by Freya Littledale. Scholastic, 1988.

The Singing Snake, written by Stefan Czernecki and Timothy Rhodes. Hyperion, 1993.
Stone Soup, written by Marcia Brown. Aladdin, 1986.
Sylvester and the Magic Pebble, written by William Steig. Simon & Schuster, 1969.
Why Mosquitos Buzz in People's Ears: A West African Tale, written by Verna Aardema. Dial, 1975.

Biographies

Abe Lincoln's Hat, written by Martha Brenner. Random House, 1994.
Action Jackson, written by Jan Greenberg. Square Fish, 2007.[b]
Cesar Chavez: The Struggle for Justice, written by Richard Griswold del Castillo. Pinata, 2008.[b]
Eleanor, written by Barbara Cooney. Penguin, 1996.
Helen Keller's Teacher, written by Margaret Davidson. Scholastic, 1965.
I Have a Dream: The Story of Martin Luther King, written by Margaret Davidson. Scholastic, 1986.
Meet Abraham Lincoln, written by Barbara Cary. Random House, 1989.
Red Bird Sings: The Story of Zitkala-Sa, Native American Author, Musician, and Activist, written by Q. L. Pearce and Gina Capaldi. Millbrook, 2011.[b]
Roberto Clemente: Pride of the Pittsburgh Pirates, written by Jonah Winter. Atheneum, 2005.[b]
Rosa Parks and the Montgomery Bus Boycott, written by Teresa Celsi. Millbrook, 1991.
Sadako and the Thousand Paper Cranes, written by Eleanor Coerr. Bantam Doubleday Dell, 1977.
Shark Lady: True Adventures of Eugenie Clark, written by Ann McGovern. Scholastic, 1978.
Sojourner Truth: Crusade for Civil Rights, written by Norman L. Macht. Chelsea House, 1992.
Talking About Bessie: The Story of Aviator Elizabeth Coleman, written by Nikki Grimes. Orchard, 2002.[i]

Award-Winning Trade Books
for Children, 2000–2014

Batchelder Award

. . . .

This award, sponsored by the American Library Association, is given to the U.S. publisher of a children's book considered to be the most outstanding of those originally published in a country other than the United States and in a language other than English and subsequently translated into English. (*www.ala.org*).

2014 Award Winner

Mister Orange, written by Truus Matti and translated by Laura Watkinson, Enchanted Lion Books.

2014 Honor Books

The Bathing Costume, or the Worst Vacation of My Life, written by Charlotte Moundlic and illustrated by Olivier Tallec, and translated by Claudia Zoe Bedrick. Enchanted Lion Books.
My Father's Arms Are a Boat, written by Stein Erik Lunde and illustrated by Øyvind Torseter, and translated by Kari Dickson. Enchanted Lion Books.
The War within These Walls, written by Aline Sax and illustrated by Caryl Strzelecki, and translated by Laura Watkinson. Eerdmans Books for Young Readers.

2013 Award Winner

My Family for the War, written by Anne C. Voorhoeve and translated by Tammi Reichel. Dial Books.

2013 Honor Books

A Game for Swallows: To Die, to Leave, to Return, written and illustrated by Zeina Abirached, and translated by Edward Gauvin. Graphic Universe.
Son of a Gun, written by Anne de Graaf, and translated by the author. Eerdmans Books for Young Readers.

2012 Award Winner

Soldier Bear, written by Bibi Dumon Tak and illustrated by Philip Hopman, and translated by Laura Watkinson. Eerdmans Books for Young Readers.

2012 Honor Book

The Lily Pond, written by Annika Thor and translated by Linda Schenck. Delacorte Press.

2011 Award Winner

A Time of Miracles, written by Anne-Laure Bondoux and translated by Y. Maudet. Delacorte Press.

2011 Honor Books

Departure Time, written by Truus Matti and translated by Nancy Forest-Flier. Namelos.
Nothing, written by Janne Teller and translated by Martin Aitken. Atheneum Books for Young Readers.

2010 Award Winner

A Faraway Island, writtten by Annika Thor and translated by Linda Schenck. Delacorte Press.

2010 Honor Books

Eidi, written by Bodil Bredsdorff and translated by Kathryn Mahaffy. Farrar, Straus & Giroux.
Big Wolf and Little Wolf, written by Nadine Brun-Cosme, illustrated by Olivier Tallec, and translated by Claudia Bedrick. Enchanted Lion Books.
Moribito II: Guardian of the Darkness, written by Nahoko Uehashi, illustrated by Yuko Shimizu, and translated Cathy Hirano. Arthur A. Levine Books.

2009 Award Winner

Moribito: Guardian of the Spirit, writtten by Nahoko Uehashi and translated by Cathy Hirano. Arthur A. Levine Books.

2009 Honor Books

Garmann's Summer, written and illustrated by Stian Hole and translated by Don Bartlett. Eerdmans Books for Young Readers.
Tiger Moon, written by Antonia Michaelis and translated by Anthea Bell. Amulet Books.

2008 Award Winner

Brave Story, written by Miyuki Miyabe and translated by Alexander O. Smith. VIZ Media.

2008 Honor Books

The Cat: Or, How I Lost Eternity, written by Jutta Richter, with illustrations by Rotraut Susanne Berner, and translated by Anna Brailovsky. Milkweed Editions.

Nicholas and the Gang, written by René Goscinny, illustrated by Jean-Jacques Sempé, and translated by Anthea Bell. Phaidon Press.

2007 Award Winner

The Pull of the Ocean, written by Jean-Claude Mourlevat and translated by Y. Maudet. Delacorte Press.

2007 Honor Books

The Killer's Tears, written by Anne-Laure Bondoux and translated by Y. Maudet. Delacorte Press.
The Last Dragon, written by Silvana De Mari and translated by Shaun Whiteside. Hyperion/Miramax.

2006 Award Winner

An Innocent Soldier, written by Josef Holub and translated by Michael Hofmann. Arthur A. Levine Books.

2006 Honor Books

Nicholas written by René Goscinny and illustrated by Jean-Jacques Sempé, and translated by Anthea Bell. Phaidon Press.
When I Was a Soldier, written by Valérie Zenatti and translated by Adriana Hunter. Bloomsbury Children's Books.

2005 Award Winner

The Shadows of Ghadames, written by Joëlle Stolz and translated by Catherine Temerson. Delacorte Press/Random House Children's Books.

2005 Honor Books

The Crow-Girl: The Children of Crow Cove, written by Bodil Bredsdorff and translated by Faith Ingwersen. Farrar Straus Giroux.
Daniel Half Human and the Good Nazi, written by David Chotjewitz and translated by Doris Orgel. Richard Jackson Books/Simon & Schuster's Atheneum Division.

2004 Award Winner

Run, Boy, Run, written by Uri Orlev and translated by Hillel Halkin. Walter Lorraine Books/Houghton Mifflin.

2004 Honor Book

The Man Who Went to the Far Side of the Moon: The Story of Apollo 11 Astronaut Michael Collins, written by Bea Uusma Schyffert and translated by Emi Guner. Chronicle Books.

2003 Award Winner

The Thief Lord, written by Cornelia Funke and translated by Oliver Latsch. Chicken House/Scholastic.

2003 Honor Book

Henrietta and the Golden Eggs, written by Hanna Johansen, illustrated by Käthi Bhend, and translated by John Barrett. David R. Godine.

2002 Award Winner

How I Became an American, written by Karin Gündisch and translated by James Skofield. Cricket Books/Carus.

2002 Honor Book

A Book of Coupons, written by Susie Morgenstern, illustrated by Serge Bloch, and translated by Gill Rosner. Viking Press.

2001 Award Winner

Samir and Yonatan, written by Daniella Carmi and translated by Yael Lotan. Arthur A. Levine Books/Scholastic Press.

2001 Honor Book

Ultimate Game, written by Christian Lehmann and translated by William Rodarmor. David R. Godine.

2000 Award Winner

The Baboon King, written by Anton Quintana and translated by John Nieuwenhuizen. Walker and Company.

2000 Honor Books

Collector of Moments, written by Quint Buchholz and translated by Peter F. Neumeyer. Farrar, Straus & Giroux.
Vendela in Venice, written by Christina Björk, illustrated by Inga-Karin Eriksson, and translated by Patricia Crampton. R & S Books.
Asphalt Angels, written by Ineke Holtwijk and translated by Wanda Boeke. Front Street.

Caldecott Medal

This award, sponsored by the Association for Library Service to Children of the American Library Association, is given to the most distinguished picture book published in the United States in the preceding year. (*www.ala.org*).

2014 Winners

Medal Winner

Locomotive, written and illustrated by Brian Floca. Atheneum Books for Young Readers.

Honor Books

Journey, written and illustrated by Aaron Becker. Candlewick Press.
Flora and the Flamingo, written and illustrated by Molly Idle. Chronicle Books.
Mr. Wuffles!, written and illustrated by David Wiesner. Clarion Books.

2013 Winners

Medal Winner

This Is Not My Hat, written and illustrated by Jon Klassen. Candlewick Press.

Honor Books

Creepy Carrots!, written by Aaron Reynolds and illustrated by Peter Brown. Simon & Schuster
   Books for Young Readers.
Extra Yarn, written by Mac Barnett and illustrated by Jon Klassen. Balzer & Bray.
Green, written and illustrated by Laura Vaccaro. Seeger Neal Porter Books.
One Cool Friend, written by Toni Buzzeo and illustrated by David Small. Dial Books for Young
   Readers.
Sleep Like a Tiger, written by Mary Logue and illustrated by Pamela Zagarenski. Houghton
   Mifflin Books for Children.

2012 Winners

Medal Winner

A Ball for Daisy, written by Chris Raschka. Schwartz & Wade Books.

Honor Books

Blackout, written by John Rocco. Disney Hyperion Books.
Grandpa Green, written by Lane Smith. Roaring Brook Press.
Me . . . Jane, written by Patrick McDonnell. Little, Brown & Company.

2011 Winners

Medal Winner

A Sick Day for Amos McGee, written by Philip C. Stead and illustrated by Erin E. Stead. Neal
   Porter Books.

Honor Books

Dave the Potter: Artist, Poet, Slave, written by Laban Carrick Hill and illustrated by Bryan
   Collier. Little, Brown & Company.
Interrupting Chicken, written by David Ezra Stein. Candlewick Press.

2010 Winners

Medal Winner

The Lion & the Mouse, written by Jerry Pinkney. Little, Brown & Company.

Honor Books

All the World, written by Liz Garton Scanlon and illustrated by Marla Frazee. Beach Lane Books.

Red Sings from Treetops: A Year in Colors, written by Joyce Sidman and illustrated by Pamela Zagarenski. Houghton Mifflin Books for Children/Houghton Mifflin Harcourt.

2009 Winners

Medal Winner

The House in the Night, written by Susan Marie Swanson and illustrated by Beth Krommes. Houghton Mifflin Company.

Honor Books

A Couple of Boys Have the Best Week Ever, written by Marla Frazee. Harcourt, Inc.

How I Learned Geography, written by Uri Shulevitz. Farrar, Straus & Giroux.

A River of Words: The Story of William Carlos Williams, written by Jen Bryant and illustrated by Melissa Sweet. Eerdmans Books for Young Readers.

2008 Winners

Medal Winner

The Invention of Hugo Cabret, written by Brian Selznick. Scholastic Press.

Honor Books

Henry's Freedom Box: A True Story from the Underground Railroad, written by Ellen Levine and illustrated by Kadir Nelson. Scholastic Press.

First the Egg, written and illustrated by Laura Vaccaro Seeger. Roaring Brook/Neal Porter Books.

The Wall: Growing Up Behind the Iron Curtain, written and illustrated by Peter Sís. Farrar/Frances Foster.

Knuffle Bunny Too: A Case of Mistaken Identity, written and illustrated by Mo Willems. Hyperion.

2007 Winners

Medal Winner

Flotsam, written by David Wiesner. Clarion Books.

Honor Books

Gone Wild: An Endangered Animal Alphabet, written by David McLimans. Walker.

Moses: When Harriet Tubman Led Her People to Freedom, written by Carole Boston Weatherford and illustrated by Kadir Nelson. Hyperion/Jump at the Sun.

2006 Winners

Medal Winner

The Hello, Goodbye Window, written by Norton Juster and illustrated by Chris Raschka. Michael di Capua Books/Hyperion Books for Children.

Honor Books

Rosa, written by Nikki Giovanni and illustrated by Bryan Collier. Henry Holt and Company.
Zen Shorts, written and illustrated by Jon J. Muth. Scholastic Press.
Hot Air: The (Mostly) True Story of the First Hot-Air Balloon Ride, written and illustrated by Marjorie Priceman. An Anne Schwartz Book/Atheneum Books for Young Readers/ Simon & Schuster.
Song of the Water Boatman and Other Pond Poems, written by Joyce Sidman and illustrated by Beckie Prange. Houghton Mifflin Company.

2005 Winners

Medal Winner

Kitten's First Full Moon, written by Kevin Henkes. Greenwillow Books/HarperCollins.

Honor Books

The Red Book, written by Barbara Lehman. Houghton Mifflin.
Coming on Home Soon, written by Jacqueline Woodson and illustrated by E. B. Lewis. G. P. Putnam's Son's/Penguin Young Readers Group.
Knuffle Bunny: A Cautionary Tale, written and illustrated by Mo Willems. Hyperion Books for Children.

2004 Winners

Medal Winner

The Man Who Walked between the Towers, written by Mordicai Gerstein. Roaring Brook Press/Millbrook Press.

Honor Books

Ella Sarah Gets Dressed, written by Margaret Chodos-Irvine. Harcourt, Inc.
What Do You Do with a Tail Like This?, written and illustrated by Steve Jenkins and Robin Page. Houghton Mifflin Company.
Don't Let the Pigeon Drive the Bus, written by Mo Willems. Hyperion.

2003 Winners

Medal Winner

My Friend Rabbit, written by Eric Rohmann. Roaring Brook Press/Millbrook Press.

Honor Books

The Spider and the Fly, written by Mary Howitt and illustrated by Tony DiTerlizzi. Simon & Schuster Books for Young Readers.
Hondo & Fabian, written by Peter McCarty. Henry Holt and Company.
Noah's Ark, written by Jerry Pinkney. SeaStar Books.

2002 Winners

Medal Winner

The Three Pigs, written by David Wiesner. Clarion Books/Houghton Mifflin.

Honor Books

The Dinosaurs of Waterhouse Hawkins, written by Barbara Kerley and illustrated by Brian Selznick. Scholastic.
Martin's Big Words: The Life of Dr. Martin Luther King, Jr., written by Doreen Rappaport and illustrated by Bryan Collier. Jump at the Sun/Hyperion.
The Stray Dog, written by Marc Simont. HarperCollins.

2001 Winners

Medal Winner

So You Want to Be President?, written by Judith St. George and illustrated by David Small. Philomel.

Honor Books

Casey at the Bat, written by Ernest Thayer and illustrated by Christopher Bing. Handprint.
Click, Clack, Moo: Cows That Type, written by Doreen Cronin and illustrated by Betsy Lewin. Simon & Schuster.
Olivia, written by Ian Falconer. Atheneum.

2000 Winners

Medal Winner

Joseph Had a Little Overcoat, written by Simms Taback. Viking.

Honor Books

A Child's Calendar, written by John Updike and illustrated by Trina Schart Hyman. Holiday House.
Sector 7, written by David Wiesner. Clarion Books.
When Sophie Gets Angry—Really, Really Angry, written by Molly Bang. Scholastic.
The Ugly Duckling, written by Hans Christian Andersen, adapted and illustrated by Jerry Pinkney. Morrow.

Carter G. Woodson Book Award (National Council for the Social Studies—Elementary Level, Grades K–6)

This award, established by the National Council for Social Studies, is given for books for young readers that depict ethnicity in the United States. The award is intended to "encourage the writing, publishing, and dissemination of outstanding social studies books for young readers that treat topics related to ethnic minorities and race relations sensitively and accurately." (*www. socialstudies.org*).

2013 Winners

Award Winner

Fifty Cents and a Dream: Young Booker T. Washington, written by Jabari Asim. Little, Brown & Company.

Honor Book

Harlem's Little Blackbird: The Story of Florence Mills, written by Renée Watson and illustrated by Christian Robinson. Random House.

2012 Winners

Award Winner

Red Bird Sings: The Story of Zitkala-ša, Native American Author, Musician, and Activist, adapted by Gina Capaldi and Q. L. Pearce. Carolrhoda Books.

Honor Book

A Nation's Hope: The Story of Boxing Legend Joe Louis, written by Matt De La Peña. Dial Books for Young Readers.

2011 Winners

Award Winner

Sit In: How Four Friends Stood Up by Sitting Down, written by Andrea Davis Pinkney. Little, Brown and Company.

Honor Book

Dave the Potter: Artist, Poet, Slave, written by Laban Carrick Hill. Little, Brown and Company.

2010 Winners

Award Winner

Shining Star: The Anna May Wong Story, written by Paula Yoo. Lee & Low Books.

Honor Book

Bad News for Outlaws: The Remarkable Life of Bass Reeves, Deputy U.S. Marshal, written by Vaunda Micheaux Nelson. Carolrhoda Books.

2009 Winners
Award Winner

Lincoln and Douglass: An American Friendship, written by Nikki Giovanni. Henry Holt and Company.

Honor Book

A Boy Named Beckoning: The True Story of Dr. Carlos Montezuma, Native American Hero, adapted and illustrated by Gina Capaldi. Carolrhoda Books.

2008 Winners
Award Winner

Louis Sockalexis: Native American Baseball Pioneer, written by Bill Wise. Lee & Low Books.

Honor Book

Surfer of the Century, written by Ellie Crowe. Lee & Low Books.

2007 Winners
Award Winner

John Lewis in the Lead: A Story of the Civil Rights Movement, written by Jim Haskins and Kathleen Benson. Lee & Low Books.

Honor Book

Gordon Parks: No Excuses, written by Ann Parr. Pelican.

2006 Winners
Award Winner

Let Them Play, written by Margot Theis Raven. Sleeping Bear Press.

Honor Book

Roberto Clemente: Pride of the Pittsburgh Pirates, written by Jonah Winter. Atheneum Books for Young Readers.

2005 Winners
Award Winner

Jim Thorpe's Bright Path, written by Joseph Bruchac. Lee & Low Books.

Honor Book

Alec's Primer, written by Mildred Pitts Walter. Vermont Folklife Center.

2004 Winners
Award Winner

Sacagawea, written by Liselotte Erdrich. Carolrhoda Books.

Honor Book

Harvesting Hope: The Story of Cesar Chavez, written by Kathleen Krull. Harcourt.

2003 Winners
Award Winner

Cesar Chavez: The Struggle for Justice/Cesar Chavez: La lucha por la justicia, written by Richard Griswold del Castillo. Pinata Books.

Honor Book

The Daring Escape of Ellen Craft, written by Cathy Moore. Carolrhoda Books.

2002 Winners
Award Winner

Coming Home: A Story of Josh Gibson, Baseball's Greatest Home Run Hitter, written by Nanette Mellage. Troll BridgeWater Books.

Honor Book

Children of the Civil Rights Era, written by Catherine A. Welch. Carolrhoda Books.

2001 Winners
Award Winner

The Sound That Jazz Makes, written by Carole Boston Weatherford. Walker & Co.

Honor Book

Children of the Relocation Camps, written by Catherine A. Welch. Carolrhoda Books.

2000 Winners
Award Winner

Through My Eyes, written by Ruby Bridges. Scholastic Press.

Honor Books

Magic Windows/Ventanas Magicas, written by Carmen Lomas Garza. Children's Book Press.
Children of the Tlingit, written by Frank Staub. Carolrhoda Books.

Coretta Scott King Author Award

This award is given to an African American author and illustrator whose children's book, published in the previous year, made an outstanding inspirational and educational contribution to literature for children and young people. (*www.ala.org*).

2014 Winners

Author Award Winner

P.S. Be Eleven, written by Rita Williams-Garcia. Amistad.

Author Honor Books

March: Book One, written by John Lewis and Andrew Aydin. Top Shelf Productions.
Darius & Twig, written by Walter Dean Myers. Amistad.
Words with Wings, written by Nikki Grimes. WordSong.

2013 Winners

Author Award Winner

Hand in Hand: Ten Black Men Who Changed America, written by Andrea Davis Pinkney. Disney Jump at the Sun.

Author Honor Books

Each Kindness, written by Jacqueline Woodson. Nancy Paulsen Books.
No Crystal Stair: A Documentary Novel of the Life and Work of Lewis Micheaux, Harlem Bookseller, written by Vaunda Micheaux Nelson. Carolrhoda Books.

2012 Winners

Author Award Winner

Heart and Soul: The Story of America and African Americans, written by Kadir Nelson. Balzer & Bray.

Author Honor Books

The Great Migration: Journey to the North, written by Eloise Greenfield. Amistad.
Never Forgotten, written by Patricia C. McKissack. Schwartz & Wade Books.

2011 Winners

Author Award Winner

One Crazy Summer, written by Rita Williams-Garcia. Amistad.

Author Honor Books

Lockdown, written by Walter Dean Myers. Amistad.
Ninth Ward, written by Jewell Parker Rhodes. Little, Brown and Company.
Yummy: The Last Days of a Southside Shorty, written by G. Neri. Lee & Low Books.

2010 Winners

Author Award Winner

Bad News for Outlaws: The Remarkable Life of Bass Reeves, Deputy U.S. Marshal, written by Vaunda Micheaux Nelson. Carolrhoda Books.

Author Honor Books

Mare's War, written by Tanita S. Davis. Knopf.

2009 Winners

Author Award Winner

We Are the Ship: The Story of Negro League Baseball, written by Kadir Nelson. Disney Jump at the Sun.

Author Honor Books

Keeping the Night Watch, written by Hope Anita Smith. Henry Holt and Company.
The Blacker the Berry, written by Joyce Carol Thomas. Joanna Cotler Books.
Becoming Billie Holiday, written by Carole Boston Weatherford. Wordsong.

2008 Winners

Author Award Winner

Elijah of Buxton, written by Christopher Paul Curtis. Scholastic.

Author Honor Books

November Blues, written by Sharon M. Draper. Atheneum Books for Young Adults.
Twelve Rounds to Glory: The Story of Muhammad Ali, written by Charles R. Smith Jr. Candlewick Press.

2007 Winners

Author Award Winner

Copper Sun, written by Sharon Draper. Simon & Schuster/Atheneum Books for Young Readers.

Author Honor Books

The Road to Paris, written by Nikki Grimes. G. P. Putnam's Sons.

2006 Winners

Author Award Winner

Day of Tears: A Novel in Dialogue, written by Julius Lester. Jump at the Sun.

Author Honor Books

Maritcha: A Nineteenth-Century American Girl, written by Tonya Bolden. Harry N. Abrams.
Dark Sons, written by Nikki Grimes. Jump at the Sun.
A Wreath for Emmett Till, written by Marilyn Nelson. Houghton Mifflin.

2005 Winners

Author Award Winner

Remember: The Journey to School Integration, written by Toni Morrison. Houghton Mifflin.

Author Honor Books

The Legend of Buddy Bush, written by Shelia P. Moses. Margaret K. McElderry Books.
Who Am I without Him?: Short Stories about Girls and the Boys in Their Lives, written by Sharon G. Flake. Jump at the Sun/Hyperion Books for Children.
Fortune's Bones: The Manumission Requiem, written by Marilyn Nelson. Front Street.

2004 Winners

Author Award Winner

The First Part Last, written by Angela Johnson. Simon & Schuster Books for Young Readers.

Author Honor Books

Days of Jubilee: The End of Slavery in the United States, written by Patricia C. McKissack and Fredrick L. McKissack. Scholastic Press.
Locomotion, written by Jacqueline Woodson. Grosset & Dunlap.
The Battle of Jericho, written by Sharon Draper. Atheneum Books for Young Readers.

2003 Winners

Author Award Winner

Bronx Masquerade, written by Nikki Grimes. Dial Books for Young Readers.

Author Honor Books

The Red Rose Box, written by Brenda Woods. G. P. Putnam's Sons.
Talkin' About Bessie: The Story of Aviator Elizabeth Coleman, written by Nikki Grimes.
   Orchard Books/Scholastic.

2002 Winners

Author Award Winner

The Land, written by Mildred Taylor. Phyllis Fogelman Books/Penguin Putnam.

Author Honor Books

Money-Hungry, written by Sharon G. Flake. Jump at the Sun/Hyperion.
Carver: A Life in Poems, written by Marilyn Nelson. Front Street.

2001 Winners

Author Award Winner
Miracle's Boys, written by Jacqueline Woodson. G. P. Putnam's Sons.

Author Honor Book

Let It Shine! Stories of Black Women Freedom Fighters, written by Andrea Davis Pinkney.
   Gulliver Books/Harcourt.

2000 Winners

Author Award Winner

Bud, Not Buddy, written by Christopher Paul Curtis. Delacorte Press.

Author Honor Book

Francie, written by Karen English. Farrar, Straus & Giroux.
Black Hands, White Sails: The Story of African-American Whalers, written by Patricia C.
   McKissack and Frederick L. McKissack. Scholastic Press.
Monster, written by Walter Dean Myers. HarperCollins.

Newbery Medal

· ·

This award is presented by the Association for Library Service to Children, a division of the American Library Association, to the author of the most distinguished contribution to American literature for children. (*www.ala.org*).

2014 Winners

Medal Winner

Flora & Ulysses: The Illuminated Adventures, written by Kate DiCamillo. Candlewick Press.

Honor Books

Doll Bones, written by Holly Black. Margaret K. McElderry Books.
The Year of Billy Miller, written by Kevin Henkes. Greenwillow Books.
One Came Home, written by Amy Timberlake. Knopf.
Paperboy, written by Vince Vawter. Delacorte Press.

2013 Winners

Medal Winner

The One and Only Ivan, written by Katherine Applegate. HarperCollins Children's Books.

Honor Books

Splendors and Glooms, written by Laura Amy Schlitz. Candlewick Press.
Bomb: The Race to Build—and Steal—the World's Most Dangerous Weapon, written by Steve Sheinkin. Flash Point/Roaring Brook Press.
Three Times Lucky, written by Sheila Turnage. Dial/Penguin Young Readers Group.

2012 Winners

Medal Winner

Dead End in Norvelt, written by Jack Gantos. Farrar, Straus & Giroux.

Honor Books

Inside Out & Back Again, written by Thanhha Lai. HarperCollins Children's Books.
Breaking Stalin's Nose, written by Eugene Yelchin. Henry Holt and Company.

2011 Winners

Medal Winner

Moon over Manifest, written by Clare Vanderpool. Delacorte Press.

Honor Books

Turtle in Paradise, written by Jennifer L. Holm. Random House Children's Books.
Heart of a Samurai, written by Margi Preus. Amulet Books.
Dark Emperor and Other Poems of the Night, written by Joyce Sidman. Houghton Mifflin Books for Children.
One Crazy Summer, written by Rita Williams-Garcia. Amistad.

2010 Winners

Medal Winner

When You Reach Me, by Rebecca Stead. Wendy Lamb Books.

Honor Books

Claudette Colvin: Twice toward Justice, by Phillip Hoose. Melanie Kroupa Books/Farrar, Straus & Giroux.
The Evolution of Calpurnia Tate, written by Jacqueline Kelly. Henry Holt and Company.
Where the Mountain Meets the Moon, written by Grace Lin. Little, Brown and Company Books for Young Readers.
The Mostly True Adventures of Homer P. Figg, written by Rodman Philbrick. Blue Sky Press.

2009 Winners

Medal Winner

The Graveyard Book, written by Neil Gaiman. HarperCollins.

Honor Books

The Underneath, written by Kathi Appelt. Atheneum Books for Young Readers.
The Surrender Tree: Poems of Cuba's Struggle for Freedom, written by Margarita Engle. Henry Holt and Company.
Savvy, written by Ingrid Law. Dial Books for Young Readers.
After Tupac & D Foster, written by Jacqueline Woodson. G. P. Putnam's Sons.

2008 Winners

Medal Winner

Good Masters! Sweet Ladies! Voices from a Medieval Village, written by Laura Amy Schlitz. Candlewick Press.

Honor Books

Elijah of Buxton, written by Christopher Paul Curtis. Scholastic.
The Wednesday Wars, written by Gary D. Schmidt. Clarion Books.
Feathers, written by Jacqueline Woodson. G. P. Putnam's Sons.

2007 Winners

Medal Winner

The Higher Power of Lucky, written by Susan Patron. Simon & Schuster/Richard Jackson.

Honor Books

Penny from Heaven, written by Jennifer L. Holm. Random House.
Hattie Big Sky, written by Kirby Larson. Delacorte Press.
Rules, written by Cynthia Lord. Scholastic.

2006 Winners

Medal Winner

Criss Cross, written by Lynne Rae Perkins. Greenwillow Books/HarperCollins.

Honor Books

Whittington, written by Alan Armstrong. Random House.
Hitler Youth: Growing Up in Hitler's Shadow, written by Susan Campbell Bartoletti. Scholas-
    tic.
Princess Academy, written by Shannon Hale. Bloomsbury Children's Books.
Show Way, written by Jacqueline Woodson. G. P. Putnam's Sons.

2005 Winners

Medal Winner

Kira-Kira, written by Cynthia Kadohata. Atheneum Books for Young Readers/Simon & Schuster.

Honor Books

Al Capone Does My Shirts, written by Gennifer Choldenko. G. P. Putnam's Sons.
The Voice That Challenged a Nation: Marian Anderson and the Struggle for Equal Rights, writ-
    ten by Russell Freedman. Clarion Books/Houghton Mifflin.
Lizzie Bright and the Buckminster Boy, written by Gary D. Schmidt. Clarion Books/Houghton
    Mifflin.

2004 Winners

Medal Winner

*The Tale of Despereaux: Being the Story of a Mouse, a Princess, Some Soup, and a Spool of
    Thread*, written by Kate DiCamillo. Candlewick Press.

Honor Books

Olive's Ocean, written by Kevin Henkes. Greenwillow Books.
An American Plague: The True and Terrifying Story of the Yellow Fever Epidemic of 1793,
    written by Jim Murphy. Clarion Books.

2003 Winners

Medal Winner

Crispin: The Cross of Lead, written by Avi. Hyperion Books for Children.

Honor Books

The House of the Scorpion, written by Nancy Farmer. Atheneum.
Pictures of Hollis Woods, written by Patricia Reilly Giff. Random House/Wendy Lamb Books.
Hoot, written by Carl Hiaasen. Knopf.
A Corner of the Universe, written by Ann M. Martin. Scholastic.
Surviving the Applewhites, written by Stephanie S. Tolan. HarperCollins.

2002 Winners

Medal Winner

A Single Shard, written by Linda Sue Park. Clarion Books/Houghton Mifflin.

Honor Books

Everything on a Waffle, written by Polly Horvath. Farrar, Straus & Giroux.
Carver: A Life In Poems, written by Marilyn Nelson. Front Street.

2001 Winners

Medal Winner

A Year Down Yonder, written by Richard Peck. Dial.

Honor Books

Hope Was Here, written by Joan Bauer. G. P. Putnam's Sons.
Because of Winn-Dixie, written by Kate DiCamillo. Candlewick Press.
Joey Pigza Loses Control, written by Jack Gantos. Farrar, Straus & Giroux.
The Wanderer, written by Sharon Creech. Joanna Cotler Books/HarperCollins.

2000 Winners

Medal Winner

Bud, Not Buddy, written by Christopher Paul Curtis. Delacorte Press.

Honor Books

Getting Near to Baby, written by Audrey Couloumbis. G. P. Putnam's Sons.
Our Only May Amelia, written by Jennifer L. Holm. HarperCollins.
26 Fairmount Avenue, written by Tomie dePaola. G. P. Putnam's Sons.

Pura Belpré Narrative Award

This award honors Latino writers and illustrators whose work best portrays, affirms, and celebrates the Latino cultural experience in a work of literature for youth. (*www.ala.org*).

2014 Winners
Medal Winner

Yaqui Delgado Wants to Kick Your Ass, written by Meg Medina. Candlewick Press.

Honor Books

The Lightning Dreamer: Cuba's Greatest Abolitionist, written by Margarita Engle. Harcourt.
The Living, written by Matt de la Peña. Delacorte Press.
Pancho Rabbit and the Coyote: A Migrant's Tale, written by Duncan Tonatiuh. Abrams Books for Young Readers.

2013 Winners
Medal Winner

Aristotle and Dante Discover the Secrets of the Universe, written by Benjamin Alire Sáenz. Simon & Schuster Books for Young Readers.

Honor Book

The Revolution of Evelyn Serrano, written by Sonia Manzano. Scholastic Press.

2012 Winners
Medal Winner

Under the Mesquite, written by Guadalupe Garcia McCall. Lee & Low Books.

Honor Books

Hurricane Dancers: The First Caribbean Pirate Shipwreck, written by Margarita Engle. Henry Holt and Company.
Maximilian and the Mystery of the Guardian Angel: A Bilingual Lucha Libre Thriller, written by Xavier Garza. Cinco Puntos Press.

2011 Winners
Medal Winner

The Dreamer, written by Pam Muñoz Ryan. Scholastic Press.

Honor Books

¡Ole! Flamenco, written by George Ancona. Lee & Low Books.
The Firefly Letters: A Suffragette's Journey to Cuba, written by Margarita Engle. Henry Holt and Company.
90 Miles to Havana, written by Enrique Flores-Galbis. Roaring Brook Press.

2010 Winners

Medal Winner

Return to Sender, written by Julia Alvarez. Knopf.

Honor Books

Diego: Bigger Than Life, by Carmen T. Bernier-Grand. Marshall Cavendish Children.
Federico García Lorca, written by Georgina Lázaro. Lectorum Publications.

2009 Winners

Medal Winner

The Surrender Tree: Poems of Cuba's Struggle for Freedom, written by Margarita Engle. Henry Holt and Company.

Honor Books

Just In Case, written by Yuyi Morales. Roaring Brook Press/Neal Porter Books.
Reaching Out, written by Francisco Jiménez. Houghton Mifflin.
The Storyteller's Candle/La velita de los cuentos, written by Lucía González. Children's Book Press.

2008 Winners

Medal Winner

The Poet Slave of Cuba: A Biography of Juan Francisco Manzano, written by Margarita Engle. Henry Holt and Company.

Honor Books

Frida: ¡Viva la vida! Long Live Life!, written by Carmen T. Bernier-Grand. Marshall Cavendish.
Martina the Beautiful Cockroach: A Cuban Folktale, written by Carmen Agra Deedy. Peachtree.
Los Gatos Black on Halloween, written by Marisa Montes. Henry Holt and Company.

2006 Winners

Medal Winner

The Tequila Worm, written by Viola Canales. Wendy Lamb Books.

Honor Books

César: ¡Sí, Se Puede! Yes, We Can!, written by Carmen T. Bernier-Grand. Marshall Cavendish.
Doña Flor: A Tall Tale about a Giant Woman with a Great Big Heart, written by Pat Mora. Knopf.
Becoming Naomi León, written by Pam Muñoz Ryan. Scholastic Press.

2004 Winners
Medal Winner

Before We Were Free, written by Julia Alvarez. Knopf.

Honor Books

Cuba 15, written by Nancy Osa. Delacorte Press.
My Diary from Here to There/Mi Diario de Aquí Hasta Allá, written by Amada Irma
    Pérez. Children's Book Press.

2002 Winners
Medal Winner

Esperanza Rising, written by Pam Munoz Ryan. Scholastic Press.

Honor Books

Breaking Through, written by Francisco Jiménez. Houghton Mifflin Company.
Iguanas in the Snow, written by Francisco X. Alarcón. Children's Book Press.

2000 Winners
Medal Winner

Under the Royal Palms: A Childhood in Cuba, written by Alma Flor Ada. Atheneum Books.

Honor Books

*From the Bellybutton of the Moon and Other Summer Poems/Del Ombligo de la Luna y Otro
    Poemas de Verano*, written by Francisco X. Alarcón. Children's Book Press.
Laughing out Loud, I Fly: Poems in English and Spanish, written by Juan Felipe Herrera.
    HarperCollins.

Robert F. Sibert Informational Book Medal

This book medal is awarded annually to the author of the most distinguished informational
book published during the preceding year. (*www.ala.org*).

2014 Winners
Medal Winner

Parrots over Puerto Rico, written by Susan L. Roth and Cindy Trumbore. Lee & Low Books.

Honor Books

A Splash of Red: The Life and Art of Horace Pippin, written by Jen Bryant. Knopf.
Look Up!: Bird-Watching in Your Own Backyard, written by Annette LeBlanc Cate. Candle-
    wick Press.

Locomotive, written by Brian Floca. Atheneum Books for Young Readers.

The Mad Potter: George E. Ohr, Eccentric Genius, written by Jan Greenberg and Sandra Jordan. Roaring Brook Press.

2013 Winners

Medal Winner

Bomb: The Race to Build—and Steal—the World's Most Dangerous Weapon, written by Steve Sheinkin. Flash Point.

Honor Books

Electric Ben: The Amazing Life and Times of Benjamin Franklin, written by Robert Byrd. Dial Books for Young Readers.

Moonbird: A Year on the Wind with the Great Survivor B95, written by Phillip M. Hoose. Farrar, Straus & Giroux Books for Young Readers.

Titanic: Voices from the Disaster, written by Deborah Hopkinson. Scholastic Press.

2012 Winners

Medal Winner

Balloons over Broadway: The True Story of the Puppeteer of Macy's Parade, written by Melissa Sweet. Houghton Mifflin Books for Children.

Honor Books

Black & White: The Confrontation between Reverend Fred L. Shuttlesworth and Eugene "Bull" Connor, written by Larry Dane Brimner. Calkins Creek.

Drawing from Memory, written by Allen Say. Scholastic Press.

The Elephant Scientist, written by Caitlin O'Connell and Donna M. Jackson. Houghton Mifflin Books for Children.

Witches!: The Absolutely True Tale of Disaster in Salem, written by Rosalyn Schanzer. National Geographic Society.

2011 Winners

Medal Winner

Kakapo Rescue: Saving the World's Strangest Parrot, written by Sy Montgomery. Houghton Mifflin Books for Children.

Honor Books

Ballet for Martha: Making Appalachian Spring, written by Jan Greenberg and Sandra Jordan. Neal Porter Books.

Lafayette and the American Revolution, written by Russell Freedman. Holiday House.

2010 Winners

Medal Winner

Almost Astronauts: 13 Women Who Dared to Dream, written by Tanya Lee Stone. Candlewick Press.

Honor Books

The Day-Glo Brothers: The True Story of Bob and Joe Switzer's Bright Ideas and Brand-New Colors, written by Chris Barton. Charlesbridge.
Moonshot: The Flight of Apollo 11, written by Brian Floca. Richard Jackson/Atheneum Books for Young Readers.
Claudette Colvin: Twice toward Justice, written by Phillip Hoose. Melanie Kroupa Books/ Farrar, Straus & Giroux.

2009 Winners

Medal Winner

We Are the Ship: The Story of Negro League Baseball by Kadir Nelson. Disney Jump at the Sun.

Honor Books

Bodies from the Ice: Melting Glaciers and the Recovery of the Past, written by James M. Deem. Houghton Mifflin Company.
What to Do about Alice?: How Alice Roosevelt Broke the Rules, Charmed the World, and Drove Her Father Teddy Crazy!, written by Barbara Kerley. Scholastic Press.

2008 Winners

Medal Winner

The Wall: Growing Up behind the Iron Curtain, written by Peter Sís. Farrar/Frances Foster.

Honor Books

Lightship, written by Brian Floca. Simon & Schuster/Richard Jackson.
Nic Bishop Spiders, written by Nic Bishop. Scholastic Nonfiction.

2007 Winners

Medal Winner

Team Moon: How 400,000 People Landed Apollo 11 on the Moon, written by Catherine Thimmesh. Houghton Mifflin.

Honor Books

Freedom Riders: John Lewis and Jim Zwerg on the Front Lines of the Civil Rights Movement, written by Ann Bausum. National Geographic.

Quest for the Tree Kangaroo: An Expedition to the Cloud Forest of New Guinea, written by Sy Montgomery. Houghton Mifflin.

To Dance: A Ballerina's Graphic Novel, written by Siena Cherson Siegel. Simon & Schuster/ Richard Jackson and Simon & Schuster/Aladdin.

2006 Winners

Medal Winner

Secrets of a Civil War Submarine: Solving the Mysteries of the H. L. Hunley, written by Sally M. Walker. Carolrhoda Books.

Honor Book

Hitler Youth: Growing Up in Hitler's Shadow, written by Susan Campbell Bartoletti. Scholastic Nonfiction.

2005 Winners

Medal Winner

The Voice That Challenged a Nation: Marian Anderson and the Struggle for Equal Rights, written by Russell Freedman. Clarion Books/Houghton Mifflin.

Honor Books

Walt Whitman: Words for America, written by Barbara Kerley and illustrated by Brian Selznick. Scholastic Press.

The Tarantula Scientist, written by Sy Montgomery and photographs by Nic Bishop. Houghton Mifflin.

Sequoyah: The Cherokee Man Who Gave His People Writing, written by James Rumford and translated into Cherokee by Anna Sixkiller Huckaby. Houghton Mifflin.

2004 Winners

Medal Winner

An American Plague: The True and Terrifying Story of the Yellow Fever Epidemic of 1793, written by Jim Murphy. Clarion Books/Houghton Mifflin.

Honor Book

I Face the Wind, written by Vicki Cobb and illustrated by Julia Gorton. HarperCollins.

2003 Winners

Medal Winner

The Life and Death of Adolf Hitler, written by James Cross Giblin. Clarion Books.

Honor Books

Six Days in October: The Stock Market Crash of 1929, written by Karen Blumenthal. Atheneum.
Hole in My Life, written by Jack Gantos. Farrar, Strauss & Giroux.
Action Jackson, written by Jan Greenberg and Sandra Jordan and illustrated by Robert Andrew Parker. Roaring Brook Press/Millbrook Press.
When Marian Sang, written by Pam Munoz Ryan and illustrated by Brian Selznick. Scholastic.

2002 Winners

Medal Winner

Black Potatoes: The Story of the Great Irish Famine, 1845–1850, written by Susan Campbell Bartoletti. Houghton Mifflin.

Honor Books

Surviving Hitler: A Boy in the Nazi Death Camps, written by Andrea Warren. HarperCollins.
Vincent van Gogh, written by Jan Greenberg and Sandra Jordan. Delacorte Press.
Brooklyn Bridge, written by Lynn Curlee. Simon & Schuster/Atheneum Books for Young Readers.

2001 Winners

Medal Winner

Sir Walter Raleigh and the Quest for El Dorado, written by Marc Aronson. Clarion Books.

Honor Books

The Longitude Prize, written by Joan Dash and illustrated by Dusan Petricic. Frances Foster Books/Farrar, Straus & Giroux.
Blizzard!: The Storm That Changed America, written by Jim Murphy. Scholastic Press.
My Season with Penguins: An Antarctic Journal, written by Sophie Webb. Houghton Mifflin.
Pedro and Me: Friendship, Loss, and What I Learned, written by Judd Winick. Henry Holt and Company.

Notable Trade Books
for Children, 2013–2014

Notable Children's Books (Association for Library Service to Children and American Library Association), 2013

The Association for Library Service to Children (ALSC) annually identifies this list of the best of the best of children's books. (*www.ala.org*).

Younger Readers: Preschool–Grade 2

And Then It's Spring, written by Julie Fogliano. Roaring Brook/Neal Porter Books.
Bear Has a Story to Tell, written by Philip C. Stead. Roaring Brook/Neal Porter Books.
Black Dog, written by Levi Pinfold. Candlewick Press/Templar.
Charley's First Night, written by Amy Hest. Candlewick Press.
Creepy Carrots!, written by Aaron Reynolds. Simon & Schuster Books for Young Readers.
Demolition, written by Sally Sutton. Candlewick Press.
Dogs on Duty, written by Dorothy Hinshaw Patent. Walker.
Dreaming Up: A Celebration of Building, written by Christy Hale. Lee & Low Books.
Extra Yarn, written by Mac Barnett. HarperCollins/Balzer & Bray.
Golden Domes and Silver Lanterns: A Muslim Book of Colors, written by Hena Khan. Chronicle.
Goldilocks and the Three Dinosaurs, written by Mo Willems. HarperCollins/Balzer & Bray.
Green, written by Laura Vaccaro Seeger. Roaring Brook/Neal Porter Books.
Hippopposites, written by Janik Coat. Appleseed.
Infinity and Me, written by Kate Hosford. Lerner/Carolrhoda Books.
Just Ducks, written by Nicola Davies. Candlewick Press.
Let's Go for a Drive!, written by Mo Willems. Hyperion Books.
Machines Go to Work in the City, written by William Low. Henry Holt and Company.
Magritte's Marvelous Hat: A Picture Book, written by D. B. Johnson. Houghton Mifflin.
Martin de Porres: The Rose in the Desert, written by Gary D. Schmidt. Clarion Books/Houghton Mifflin.
More, written by I. C. Springman. Houghton Mifflin.

Nighttime Ninja, written by Barbara DaCosta. Little, Brown and Company.

Oh, No!, written by Candace Fleming. Random/Schwartz & Wade.

One Cool Friend, written by Toni Buzzeo. Dial/Penguin.

One Special Day: A Story for Big Brothers and Sisters, written by Lola M. Schaefer. Disney/Hyperion.

Penny and Her Doll, written by Kevin Henkes. Greenwillow.

Pete the Cat and His Four Groovy Buttons, written by Eric Litwin. HarperCollins.

Rabbit and Robot: The Sleepover, written by Cece Bell. Candlewick Press.

Sleep Like a Tiger, written by Mary Logue. Houghton Mifflin.

This Is Not My Hat, written by Jon Klassen. Candlewick Press.

This Moose Belongs to Me, written by Oliver Jeffers. Philomel/Penguin.

Up, Tall, and High!, written by Ethan Long. G. P. Putnam's Sons/Penguin.

Z Is for Moose, written by Kelly Bingham. Greenwillow.

Middle Readers: Grades 3–5

Abraham Lincoln and Frederick Douglass: The Story behind an American Friendship, written by Russell Freedman. Clarion Books/Houghton Mifflin.

The Beetle Book, written by Steve Jenkins. Houghton Mifflin.

A Black Hole Is Not a Hole, written by Carolyn Cinami DeCristofano. Charlesbridge.

Bomb: The Race to Build—and Steal—the World's Most Dangerous Weapon, written by Steve Sheinkin. Roaring Brook/Flash Point.

Brothers at Bat: The True Story of an Amazing All-Brother Baseball Team, written by Audrey Vernick. Clarion Books/Houghton Mifflin.

Chuck Close: Face Book, written by Chuck Close. Abrams.

Each Kindness, written by Jacqueline Woodson. Penguin/Nancy Paulsen.

Electric Ben: The Amazing Life and Times of Benjamin Franklin, written by Robert Byrd. Dial/Penguin.

George Bellows: Painter with a Punch!, written by Robert Burleigh. Abrams.

Helen's Big World: The Life of Helen Keller, written by Doreen Rappaport and illustrated by Matt Tavares. Disney/Hyperion.

Iceberg, Right Ahead!: The Tragedy of the Titanic, written by Stephanie Sammartino McPherson. Lerner/Twenty-First Century.

In a Glass Grimmly, written by Adam Gidwitz. Dutton/Penguin.

Island: A Story of the Galápagos, written by Jason Chin. Roaring Brook/Neal Porter Books.

Liar & Spy, written by Rebecca Stead. Random/Wendy Lamb Books.

Lulu and the Duck in the Park, written by Hilary McKay. Albert Whitman.

May B., written by Caroline Starr Rose. Random/Schwartz & Wade.

The Mighty Mars Rovers: The Incredible Adventures of Spirit and Opportunity, written by Elizabeth Rusch. Houghton Mifflin.

Moonbird: A Year on the Wind with the Great Survivor B95, written by Phillip M. Hoose. Macmillan/Farrar.

The One and Only Ivan, written by Katherine Applegate. HarperCollins/Harper.

See You at Harry's, written by Jo Knowles. Candlewick Press.

Splendors and Glooms, written by Laura Amy Schlitz. Candlewick Press.

Starry River of the Sky, written by Grace Lin. Little, Brown and Company.

Three Times Lucky, written by Sheila Turnage. Dial/Penguin.

Titanic: Voices from the Disaster, written by Deborah Hopkinson. Scholastic Press.

Twelve Kinds of Ice, written by Ellen Bryan Obed. Houghton Mifflin.

Unspoken: A Story from the Underground Railroad, written by Henry Cole. Scholastic Press.
Wonder, written by R. J. Palacio. Knopf.
Zombie Makers: True Stories of Nature's Undead, written by Rebecca L. Johnson. Lerner/ Millbrook.

All Ages

Little Bird, written by Germano Zullo. Enchanted Lion.
National Geographic Book of Animal Poetry: 200 Poems with Photographs That Squeak, Soar, and Roar!, edited by J. Patrick Lewis. National Geographic.
Step Gently Out, written by Helen Frost. Candlewick Press.
The Year Comes Round: Haiku through the Seasons, written by Sid Farrar. Albert Whitman.
Water Sings Blue: Ocean Poems, written by Kate Coombs. Chronicle.

Children's Choice Reading List (International Reading Association and Children's Book Council), 2013

The International Reading Association and the Children's Book Council cosponsor this award, which has children evaluate and write reviews of their favorite books of the year.

Grades K–2

Amelia Bedelia's First Vote, written by Herman Parish. HarperCollins Children's Books/ Greenwillow.
Back to Front and Upside Down, written by Claire Alexander. Eerdmans Books for Young Readers.
Bad Apple: A Tale of Friendship, written by Edward Hemingway. Penguin Young Readers Group.
Bailey at the Museum, written by Harry Bliss. Scholastic Press.
Bedtime for Monsters, written by Ed Vere. Henry Holt Books for Young Readers.
Big Mean Mike, written by Michelle Knudsen. Candlewick Press.
The Duckling Gets a Cookie!?, written by Mo Willems. Hyperion Books for Children.
Every Cowgirl Loves a Rodeo, written by Rebecca Janni. Dial Books for Young Readers.
The Fly Flew In, written by David Catrow. Holiday House.
Frog and Fly: Six Slurpy Stories, written by Jeff Mack. Philomel.
Goldilocks and the Three Dinosaurs, written by Mo Willems. HarperCollins Children's Books.
Good News, Bad News, written by Jeff Mack. Chronicle.
I Know a Wee Piggy, written by Kim Norman. Dial Books for Young Readers.
I'll Save You Bobo!, written by Eileen Rosenthal. Simon & Schuster.
Ladybug Girl and Bingo, written by Jacky Davis. Dial Books for Young Readers.
Lenore Finds a Friend: A True Story from Bedlam Farm, written by Jon Katz. Henry Holt Books for Young Readers.
Library Mouse: A Museum Adventure, written by Daniel Kirk. Abrams Books for Young Readers.
Little Dog Lost: The True Story of a Brave Dog Named Baltic, written by Mônica Carnesi. Nancy Paulsen Books.
Llama Llama Time to Share, written by Anna Dewdney. Viking Children's Books.

Mice on Ice, written by Rebecca Emberley and Ed Emberley. Holiday House.
Miss Fox's Class Gets It Wrong, written by Eileen Spinelli. Albert Whitman & Company.
Nighttime Ninja, written by Barbara DaCosta. Little, Brown Books for Young Readers.
Otto the Book Bear, written by Katie Cleminson. Disney/Hyperion.
Pete the Cat and His Four Groovy Buttons, written by Eric Litwin. HarperCollins Children's Books.
Pig Has a Plan, written by Ethan Long. Holiday House.
Piggy Bunny, written by Rachel Vail. Feiwel & Friends.
Plant a Kiss, written by Amy Krouse Rosenthal. HarperCollins Children's Books.
Rat and Roach: Friends to the End, written by David Covel. Viking Children's Books.
Secret Agent Splat!, written by Rob Scotton. HarperCollins Children's Books.
Señorita Gordita, written by Helen Ketteman. Albert Whitman & Company.
Silly Doggy!, written by Adam Stower. Orchard/Scholastic Press.
The Three Ninja Pigs, written by Corey Rosen Schwartz. Penguin Young Readers Group.
Tyler Makes Pancakes!, written by Tyler Florence. HarperCollins Children's Books.

Young Readers (Grades 3–4)

5,000 Awesome Facts (about Everything!), written by National Geographic Kids. National Geographic Children's Books.
Aaron Rodgers and the Green Bay Packers: Super Bowl XLV, written by Michael Sandler. Bearport Publishing.
Another Brother, written by Matthew Cordell. Feiwel & Friends.
Bad Kitty for President, written by Nick Bruel. Roaring Brook.
Bully, written by Patricia Polacco. Penguin Young Readers Group.
Dear Cinderella, written by Mary Jane Kensington and Marian Moore. Orchard/Scholastic Press.
Dolphins in the Navy, written by Meish Goldish. Bearport Publishing.
Freaky-Strange Buildings, written byMichael Sandler. Bearport Publishing.
Garmann's Secret, written by Stian Hole. Eerdmans Books for Young Readers.
Get the Scoop on Animal Poop! From Lions to Tapeworms: 251 Cool Facts about Scat, Frass, Dung, and More!, written by Dawn Cusick. Imagine.
Giants Beware!, written by Jorge Aguirre. First Second.
Great Dane: Gentle Giant, written by Stephen Person. Bearport Publishing.
Homer, written by Diane deGroat and Shelley Rotner. Orchard/Scholastic Press.
Illusionology: The Secret Science of Magic, written by Albert Schafer. Candlewick Press.
Judy Moody and the Bad Luck Charm, written by Megan McDonald. Candlewick Press.
Just Joking: 300 Hilarious Jokes, Tricky Tongue Twisters, and Ridiculous Riddles, written by National Geographic Kids. National Geographic Children's Books.
Kevin Durant, written by Michael Sandler. Bearport Publishing.
Knuckle & Potty Destroy Happy World, written by James Proimos. Christy Ottaviano Books.
Last Laughs: Animal Epitaphs, written by J. Patrick Lewis and Jane Yolen. Charlesbridge.
Looking at Lincoln, written by Maira Kalman. Nancy Paulsen Books.
Max Goes to the Moon: A Science Adventure with Max the Dog, written by Jeffrey Bennett. Big Kid Science.
The Monster Returns, written by Peter McCarty. Henry Holt Books for Young Readers.
My Pop-Up World Atlas, written by Anita Ganeri. Templar.
Pigmares: Porcine Poems of the Silver Screen, written by Doug Cushman. Charlesbridge.
Pluto Visits Earth!, written by Steve Metzger. Orchard/Scholastic Press.

Quiz Whiz: 1,000 Super Fun, Mind-Bending, Totally Awesome Trivia Questions, written by National Geographic Kids. National Geographic Children's Books.

Saving Animals after Tornadoes, written by Stephen Person. Bearport Publishing.

Stupendous Sports Stadiums, written by Michael Sandler. Bearport Publishing.

Surviving the Hindenburg, written by Larry Verstraete. Sleeping Bear.

Third Grade Angels, written by Jerry Spinelli. Arthur Levine/Scholastic.

Touch the Sky: Alice Coachman, Olympic High Jumper, written by Ann Malaspina. Albert Whitman & Company.

Teachers' Choice Reading List (International Reading Association and Children's Book Council), 2013

Since 1989, the Teachers' Choice project has developed an annual annotated reading list of new books that encourage young people to read. These books are chosen by a cross-section of teachers throughout the United States. (*www.reading.org*).

Primary Readers: Grades K–2 (Ages 5–8)

A Leaf Can Be . . ., written by Laura Purdie Salas. Lerner.

And Then It's Spring, written by Julie Fogliano. Macmillan.

Body Actions, written by Shelley Rotner. Holiday House.

Chopsticks, written by Amy Krouse Rosenthal. Disney/Hyperion.

Creepy Carrots!, written by Aaron Reynolds. Simon & Schuster.

Green, written by Laura Vaccaro Seeger. Macmillan.

How Many Jelly Beans?: A Giant Book of Giant Numbers!, written by Andrea Menotti. Chronicle.

Otto the Book Bear, written by Katie Cleminson. Disney/Hyperion.

Plant a Little Seed, written by Bonnie Christensen. Macmillan.

Rocket Writes a Story, written by Tad Hills. Random House.

Intermediate Readers: Grades 3–5 (Ages 8–11)

The Beetle Book, written by Steve Jenkins. Houghton Mifflin.

The Boy Who Harnessed the Wind, written by William Kamkwamba and Bryan Mealer. Penguin.

Brothers at Bat: The True Story of an Amazing All-Brother Baseball Team, written by Audrey Vernick. Clarion Books.

Dogs on Duty: Soldiers' Best Friends on the Battlefield and Beyond, written by Dorothy Hinshaw Patent. Bloomsbury Walker.

Each Kindness, written by Jacqueline Woodson. Penguin.

I, Too, Am America, written by Langston Hughes. Simon & Schuster.

Rachel Carson and Her Book That Changed the World, written by Laurie Lawlor. Holiday House.

A Rock Is Lively, written by Dianna Hutts Aston. Chronicle.

A Strange Place to Call Home: The World's Most Dangerous Habitats and the Animals That Call Them Home, written by Marilyn Singer. Chronicle.

Survival at 120 Above, written by Debbie S. Miller. Bloomsbury Walker.

Notable Social Studies Trade Books for Young People (National Council for the Social Studies), 2013

The books that appear in these annotated book lists are evaluated and selected by a Book Review Committee appointed by the National Council for the Social Studies (NCSS) and assembled in cooperation with the Children's Book Council (CBC). (*www.socialstudies.org*).

Abraham Lincoln and Frederick Douglass: The Story Behind an American Friendship, written by Russell Freedman. Clarion Books.

From the Good Mountain: How Gutenberg Changed the World, written by James Rumford. Flash Point.

Hand in Hand: Ten Black Men Who Changed America, written by Andrea Davis Pinkney and illustrated by Brian Pinkney. Disney Jump at the Sun.

Barnum's Bones, written by Tracy Fern and illustrated by Boris Kulikov. Margaret Ferguson Books.

George Bellow: Painter with a Punch, written by Robert Burleigh. Abrams Books for Young Readers.

His Name was Raoul Wallenberg: Courage, Rescue, and Mystery during World War II, written by Louise W. Borden. Houghton Mifflin Harcourt Children's Book Group.

I Am Helen Keller, written by Grace Norwich. Scholastic Reference.

Looking at Lincoln, written by Maira Kalman. Nancy Paulsen Books.

Mrs. Harkness and the Panda, written by Alicia Potter and illustrated by Melissa Sweet. Knopf Books for Young Readers/Random House Children's Books.

Jazz Age Josephine: Dancer, Singer—Who's That, Who?: Why That's MISS Josephine Baker, to You!, written by Jonah Winter and illustrated by Marjorie Priceman. Simon & Schuster Children's Publishing/Atheneum.

Monsieur Marceau: Actor without Words, written by Leda Schubert and illustrated by Gerard DuBois. Flash Point.

Noah Webster and His Words, written by Jeri Chase Ferris and illustrated by Vincent X. Kirsch. Houghton Mifflin Harcourt Children's Book Group.

Stolen into Slavery, written by Judith Fradin and Dennis Fradin. National Geographic Children's Book.

Temple Grandin: How the Girl Who Loved Cows Embraced Autism and Changed the World, written by Sy Montgomery, foreword by Temple Grandin. Houghton Mifflin Harcourt Children's Book Group.

Touch the Sky: Alice Coachman, Olympic High Jumper, written by Ann Malaspina and illustrated by Eric Velasquez. Albert Whitman & Company.

Black Gold: The Story of Oil in Our Lives, written by Albert Marrin. Knopf Books for Young Readers/Random House Children's Books.

Dear Blue Sky, written by Mary Sullivan. Nancy Paulsen Books.

Kizzy Ann Stamps, written by Jeri Watts. Candlewick Press.

Personal Effects, written by E. M. Kokie. Candlewick Press.

The Pregnancy Project: A Memoir, written by Gaby Rodriguez with Jenna Glatzer. Simon & Schuster Children's Publishing.

The Boy Who Harnessed the Wind, written by William Kamkwamba and Brian Mealer and illustrated by Elizabeth Zunon. Dial.

The Camping Trip that Changed America: Theodore Roosevelt, John Muir, and Our National Parks, written by Barb Rosenstock and illustrated by Mordechai Gerstein. Dial.

Miss Sally Ann and the Panther, written by Bobbi Miller and illustrated by Megan Lloyd. Holiday House.

Starry River of the Sky, written by Grace Lin. Brown Books for Young Readers.

The Wooden Sword: A Jewish Folktale from Afghanistan, written by Ann Redisch Stampler and illustrated by Carol Liddiment. Albert Whitman and Company.

Saving Animals from Oil Spills, written by Stephen Person and illustrated with photographs. Bearport Publishing.

These Bees Count!, written by Alison Formento and illustrated by Sarah Snow. Albert Whitman and Company.

Timeless Thomas: How Thomas Edison Changed Our Lives, written by Gene Barretta. Christy Ottaviano Books.

The Glass Collector, written by Anna Perera. Albert Whitman Teen.

Laugh with the Moon, written by Shana Burg. Delacorte Books for Young Readers/Random House Children's Books.

Outcasts United: The Story of a Refugee Soccer Team That Changed a Town, written by Warren St. John, Delacorte Books for Young Readers/Random House Children's Books.

Hanging Off Jefferson's Nose: Growing Up on Mount Rushmore, written by Tina Nichols Coury and illustrated by Sally Wern Comport. Dial.

My Heart Will Not Sit Down, written by Mara Rockliff. Knopf Books for Young Readers/Random House Children's Books.

The Story of Silk: From Worm Spit to Woven Scarves, written by Richard Sobol. Candlewick Press.

Their Skeletons Speak: Kennewick Man and the Paleoamerican World, written by Sally M. Walker and Douglas W. Owsley. Carolrhoda Books.

A Thunderous Whisper, written by Christina Diaz Gonzalez. Knopf Books for Young Readers/Random House Children's Books.

Tua and the Elephant, written by R. P. Harris and illustrated by Taeeun Yoo. Chronicle Books.

Brothers at Bat, written by Audrey Vernick and illustrated by Steven Salerno. Clarion Books.

Crow, written by Barbara Wright. Random House Books for Young Readers.

Discovering Black America: From the Age of Exploration to the Twenty-First Century, written by Lind Tarrant-Reid. Abrams Books for Young Readers.

Ellen's Broom, written by Kelly Starling Lyons and illustrated by Daniel Minter. Putnam.

The Great Molasses Flood: Boston, 1919, written by Deborah Kops and illustrated with archival photographs. Charlesbridge.

Here Come the Girl Scouts!, written by Shana Corey and illustrated by Hadley Hooper. Scholastic Press.

Fifty Cents and a Dream: Young Booker T. Washington, written by Jabari Asim and illustrated by Bryan Collier. Little, Brown Books for Young Readers.

Harlem's Little Blackbird: The Story of Florence Mills, written by Renee Watson. Random House Books for Young Readers.

I Lay My Stitches Down: Poems of America Slavery, written by Cynthia Grady and illustrated by Michele Wood. Eerdmans Books for Young Readers.

The Impossible Rescue: The True Story of an Amazing Arctic Adventure, written by Martin W. Sandler. Candlewick Press.

Marching to the Mountaintop, written by Ann Bausum. National Geographic Children's Books.

Stars in the Shadows: The Negro League All-Star Game of 1934, written by Charles R. Smith Jr., and illustrated by Frank Morrison. Simon & Schuster Children's Publishing/Atheneum.

Jump into the Sky, written by Shelley Pearsall. Knopf Books for Young Readers/Random House Children's Books.

The Split History of the Civil War: A Perspectives Flip Book, written by Stephanie Fitzgerald and illustrated with prints and photographs. Compass Point Books.

Tracks, written by Diane Lee Wilson. Simon & Schuster Children's Publishing/Margaret K. McElderry.

Unspoken: A Story From the Underground Railroad, written by Henry Cole. Scholastic Press.

Walking on the Earth and Touching the Sky: Poetry and Prose by Lakota Youth at Red Cloud Indian School, edited by Timothy P. McLaughlin, foreword by Joseph Marshall III, and illustrated by S. D. Nelson. Abrams Books for Young Readers.

We March, written by Shane W. Evans. Neal Porter Books.

The Giant and How He Humbugged America, written by Jim Murphy. Scholastic Press.

Master of Deceit: J. Edgar Hoover and America in the Age of Lies, written by Marc Aronson. Candlewick Press.

A Street through Time: A 12,000-Year Walk through History, illustrated by Steve Noon. DK Publishing.

Glory Be, written by Augusta Scattergood. Scholastic Press.

The Lions of Little Rock, written by Kristin Levine. Putnam.

October Mourning: A Song for Matthew Shepard, written by Leslea Newman. Candlewick Press.

I, Too, An American, written by Langston Hughes and illustrated by Brian Collier. Simon & Schuster Children's Publishing.

Now, written by Morris Gleitzman. Henry Holt Books for Young Readers.

A Path of Stars, written by Anne Sibley O'Brien. Charlesbridge.

Tea Cakes for Tosh, written by Kelly Starling Lyons and illustrated by E. B. Lewis. Putnam.

The Quiet Place, written by Sarah Stewart and illustrated by David Small. Margaret Ferguson Books.

Zayde Comes to Live, written by Sheri Sinykin and illustrated by Kristina Swarner. Peachtree Publishers.

The Mountaintop: My Journey through the Civil Rights Movement, written by Charlayne Hunter-Gault. Flash Point.

The Revolution of Evelyn Serrano, written by Sonia Manzano. Scholastic Press.

A Beautiful Lie, written by Irfan Master. Albert Whitman Teen.

Bomb: The Race to Build—and Steal—the World's Most Dangerous Weapon, written by Steve Sheinkin. Flash Point.

Golden Domes and Silver Lanterns: A Muslim Book of Colors, written by Hena Khan and illustrated by Mehdokht Amini. Chronicle Books.

Beyond Courage: The Untold Story of Jewish Resistance during the Holocaust, written by Doreen Rappaport. Candlewick Press.

Code Name Verity, written by Elizabeth Wein. Disney/Hyperion.

Hands around the Library: Protecting Egypt's Treasured Books, written by Karen Legget Abouraya and illustrated by Susan L. Roth. Dial.

My Family for the War, written by Anne C. Voorhoeve. Dial.

Outstanding Science Trade Books for Students K–12 (National Science Teachers Association; Books Published in 2013)

The books that appear in these lists are selected as outstanding children's science trade books. They are chosen by a book review panel appointed by the National Science Teachers Association (NSTA) and assembled in cooperation with the Children's Book Council (CBC). (*www.nsta.org*).

The Animal Book, written by DK Publishing. DK Publishing.

The Animal Book, written by Steve Jenkins. Houghton Mifflin Harcourt.

Animals Upside Down, written by Steve Jenkins and Robin Page. Houghton Mifflin Harcourt.

Best Foot Forward, written by Ingo Arndt. Holiday House.

Beyond the Solar System, written by Mary Kay Carson. Chicago Review Press.

Cougar, written by Stephen Person. Bearport Publishing.

The Dolphins of Shark Bay, written by Pamela S. Turner. Houghton Mifflin Harcourt.

A Dragonfly's Life, written by Ellen Lawrence. Bearport Publishing.

The Eagles Are Back, written by Jean Craighead George. Penguin/Dial.

Eat Like a Bear, written by April Pulley Sayre. Macmillan Children's/Henry Holt Books for Young Readers.

Eight Dolphins of Katrina, written by Janet Wyman Coleman. Houghton Mifflin Harcourt.

Electrical Wizard, written by Elizabeth Rusch. Candlewick Press.

Eruption!, written by Elizabeth Rusch. Houghton Mifflin Harcourt.

Ferdinand Fox's First Summer, written by Mary Holland. Sylvan Dell.

Flight of the Honey Bee, written by Raymond Huber. Candlewick Press.

Frog Song, written by Brenda Z. Guiberson. Macmillan Children's/Henry Holt Books for Young Readers.

Giant Pacific Octopus, written by Leon Gray. Bearport Publishing.

Here Come the Humpbacks!, written by April Pulley Sayre. Charlesbridge.

Hide-and-Seek Science, written by Emma Stevenson. Holiday House.

Lifetime, written by Lola M. Schaefer. Chronicle Books.

Lives of Scientists, written by Kathleen Krull. Houghton Mifflin Harcourt.

The Long, Long Journey, written by Sandra Markle. Lerner/Millbrook Press.

Meat-Eating Plants, written by Ellen Lawrence. Bearport Publishing.

National Geographic Kids Bird Guide of North America, written by Jonathan Alderfer. National Geographic Society.

National Geographic Kids First Big Book of the Ocean, written by Catherine D. Hughes. National Geographic Society.

Next Time You See a Firefly, written by Emily Morgan. NSTA Kids.

Next Time You See a Pill Bug, written by Emily Morgan. NSTA Kids.

Next Time You See a Sunset, written by Emily Morgan. NSTA Kids.

No Monkeys, No Chocolate, written by Melissa Stewart and Allen Young. Charlesbridge.

Ocean Counting, written by Janet Lawler. National Geographic Society.

On the Move, written by Scotti Cohn. Sylvan Dell.

One Minute Mysteries, written by Eric Yoder and Natalie Yoder. Science, Naturally!

Papa's Mechanical Fish, written by Candace Fleming. Margaret Ferguson Books.

A Place for Turtles, written by Melissa Stewart. Peachtree Publishers.

Primates, written by Jim Ottaviani. Macmillan Children's/First Second Roaring Brook Press.

Roseate Spoonbill, written by Stephen Person. Bearport Publishing.

Scaly Spotted Feathered Frilled, written by Catherine Thimmesh. Houghton Mifflin Harcourt.

See What a Seal Can Do, written by Chris Butterworth. Candlewick Press.

Seymour Simon's Extreme Oceans, written by Seymour Simon. Chronicle Books.

Snow School, written by Sandra Markle. Charlesbridge.

Something Stinks, written by Gail Hedrick. Tumblehome Learning.

Stripes of All Types, written by Susan Stockdale. Peachtree Publishers.

Stronger Than Steel, written by Bridget Heos. Houghton Mifflin Harcourt.

The Tapir Scientist, written by Sy Montgomery. Houghton Mifflin Harcourt.

Things That Float and Things That Don't, written by David A. Adler. Holiday House.

Too Hot? Too Cold?, written by Caroline Arnold. Charlesbridge.

Tracking Tyrannosaurs, written by Christopher Sloan. National Geographic Society.

Ultimate Bugopedia, written by Darlyne Murawski and Nancy Honovich. National Geographic Society.

Up, Up in a Balloon, written by Lawrence F. Lowery. NSTA Kids.

Volcano Rising, written by Elizabeth Rusch. Charlesbridge.

What If You Had Animal Teeth!?, written by Sandra Markle. Scholastic Press.

What's In There?, written by Robie H. Harris. Candlewick Press.

When Rivers Burned, written by Linda Crotta Brennan. Apprentice Shop Books.

Who Says Women Can't Be Doctors?, written by Tanya Lee Stone. Christy Ottaviano Books.

Yummy!, written by Shelley Rotner and Sheila M. Kelly. Holiday House.

References

Adams, M. J. (2010–2011). Advancing our students' language and literacy: The challenge of complex texts. *American Educator, 34*(4), 3–11, 53.

Adams, M. J. (2011). The relationship between alphabetic basics, word recognition, and reading. In S. J. Samuels & A. E. Farstrup (Eds.), *What research has to say about reading instruction* (4th ed., pp. 4–24). Newark, DE: International Reading Association.

Adler, D. A. (2004). *Cam Jansen and the mystery of the stolen diamonds.* New York: Puffin.

Allington, R. L. (1983). Fluency: The neglected reading goal. *The Reading Teacher, 36,* 556–561.

Allington, R. L. (1991). Children who find learning to read difficult: School responses to diversity. In E. H. Hiebert (Ed.), *Literacy for a diverse society: Perspectives, practices, and policies* (pp. 237–252). New York: Teachers College Press.

Applegate, M. D., Applegate, A. J., & Modla, V. B. (2009). "She's my best reader; she just can't comprehend": Studying the relationship between fluency and comprehension. *The Reading Teacher, 62,* 512–521.

Ash, G. E., Kuhn, M. R., & Walpole, S. (2009). Analyzing "inconsistencies" in practice: Teachers' continued use of round robin reading. *Reading and Writing Quarterly, 25,* 87–103.

Averill, E. (1988). *The fire cat.* New York: HarperCollins.

Aylesworth, J. (1994). *The folks in the valley: A Pennsylvania Dutch ABC.* New York: HarperCollins.

Barnes, D. (2008). *Ruby and the Booker Boys #1: Brand new school.* New York: Scholastic.

Barrett, J. (1978). *Cloudy with a chance of meatballs.* New York: Atheneum Books.

Barrows, A. (2007). *Ivy and Bean.* San Francisco: Chronicle Books.

Bear, D. R., Invernizzi, M. R., Templeton, S., & Johnston, F. R. (2011). *Words their way: Word study for phonics, vocabulary, and spelling instruction* (5th ed.). Boston: Pearson.

Beauchat, K. A., Blamey, K. L., & Walpole, S. (2010). *The building blocks of preschool success.* New York: Guilford Press.

Begeny, J. C., Krouse, H. E., Ross, S. G., & Mitchell, R. C. (2009). Increasing elementary-aged students' reading fluency with small-group interventions: A comparison of repeated reading, listening passage preview, and listening only strategies. *Journal of Behavioral Education, 18*(3), 211–228.

Benjamin, R. G., & Schwanenflugel, P. J. (2010). Text complexity and oral reading prosody in young readers. *Reading Research Quarterly, 45,* 388–404.

Benjamin, R. G., Schwanenflugel, P. J., Meisinger, E. B., Groff, C., Kuhn, M. R., & Steiner, L. (2013). A spectrographically grounded scale for evaluating reading expressiveness. *Reading Research Quarterly, 48*, 105–133.

Betts, E. A. (1946). *Foundations of reading instruction*. New York: American Book.

Biemiller, A. (2003). Oral comprehension sets the ceiling on reading comprehension. *American Educator, 27*(1), 23, 44.

Blade, A. (2007). *Beast quest: Ferno the fire dragon*. New York: Scholastic.

Bonsall, C. (1982). *The case of the dumb bells*. New York: HarperCollins.

Bradley, B. A., & Jones, J. (2007). Sharing alphabet books in early childhood classrooms. *The Reading Teacher, 60*(5), 452–463.

Buckley, M. (2007). *The fairy tale detectives (The Sisters Grimm, book 1)*. New York: Abrams.

Cannon, J. (2008). *Stellaluna*. New York: Scholastic.

Carney, E. (2010). *Bats! (National Geographic Readers Series)*. Washington, DC: National Geographic Society.

Casteel, C. A. (1988). Effects of chunked reading among learning disabled students: An experimental comparison of computer and traditional chunked passages. *Journal of Educational Technology Systems, 17*(2), 115–121.

Cazet, D. (2003). *Minnie and Moo and the potato from Planet X*. New York: HarperCollins.

Chall, J. S. (1996). *Stages of reading development* (2nd ed.). Fort Worth, TX: Harcourt Brace.

Chomsky, C. (1976). After decoding: What? *Language Arts, 53*, 288–296.

Ciardi, J. (1962). *You read to me, I'll read to you*. New York: HarperCollins.

Clay, M. M. (2000). *Concepts about print: What have children learned about the way we print language?* Portsmouth, NH: Heinemann.

Clay, M. M. (2006). *An observation survey of early literacy achievement* (2nd ed.). Portsmouth, NH: Heinemann.

Cleary, B. (2013). *Beezus and Ramona*. New York: HarperCollins.

Cleary, B. (2014). *Henry Huggins*. New York: HarperCollins.

Cole, B. (1986). *The giant's toe*. New York: Farrar, Straus & Giroux.

Common Core State Standards Initiative (2012). *English language arts standards*. Available at *www.corestandards.org/ELA-Literacy*.

Cosby, B. (1997). *The best way to play: A Little Bill book for beginning readers*. New York: Cartwheel.

Cromer, W. (1970). The difference model: A new explanation for some reading difficulties. *Journal of Educational Psychology, 61*, 471–483.

Coville, B. (2007). *Aliens ate my homework*. New York: Aladdin.

Cunningham, A. E., & Stanovich, K. E. (1998). What reading does for the mind. *American Educator, 22*, 1–8.

Deno, S. L., & Marston, D. (2006). Curriculum-based measurement of oral reading: An indicator of growth in fluency. In S. J. Samuels & A. E. Farstrup (Eds.), *What research has to say about fluency instruction* (pp. 179–203). Newark, DE: International Reading Association.

Dougherty Johnson, S., & Kuhn, M. R. (2013). Automaticity versus fluency: Developing essential literacy abilities with print. In B. M. Taylor & N. K. Duke (Eds.), *Handbook of effective literacy instruction: Research-based practice K–8* (pp. 191–222). New York: Guilford Press.

Dowhower, S. L. (1989). Repeated reading: Research into practice. *The Reading Teacher, 42*, 502–507.

Draper, S. M. (2011). *The buried bones mystery (Clubhouse Mysteries)*. New York: Aladdin.

Edwards, P. A., Paratore, J. R., & Roser, N. L. (2009). Family literacy: Recognizing cultural significance. In L. M. Morrow, R. Rueda, & D. Lapp (Eds.), *Handbook of research on literacy and diversity* (pp. 77–96). New York: Guilford Press.

Ehri, L. (1995). Phases of development in learning to recognize words by sight. *Journal of Research in Reading, 18*, 116–125.

Erekson, J. (2003, May). *Prosody: The problem of expression in fluency.* Paper presented at the annual meeting of the International Reading Association, Orlando, FL.

Faulkner, W. (2012). *Absalom, Absalom!* New York: Modern Library Edition.

Flack, M. (1931). *Angus and the cat.* New York: Doubleday.

Fleischman, P. (1985). *I am Phoenix: Poems for two voices.* New York: HarperCollins.

Fleischman, P. (2004). *Joyful noise: Poems for two voices.* New York: HarperCollins.

Fleischman, P. (2008). *Big talk: Poems for four voices.* Somerville, MA: Candlewick Press.

Fountas, I. C., & Pinnell, G. S. (1999). *Matching books to readers: Using leveled books in guided reading, K–3.* Portsmouth, NH: Heinemann.

Franco, B. (2009). *Messing around on the monkey bars: And other school poems for two voices.* Somerville, MA: Candlewick Press.

Friddell, C. (2010). *Goliath: Hero of the Great Baltimore Fire.* Ann Arbor, MI: Sleeping Bear Press.

Fuchs, D., & Fuchs, L. S. (l998). Researchers and teachers working together to adapt instruction for diverse learners. *Learning Disabilities Research and Practice, 13*, 126–137.

Fuchs, L. S., & Fuchs, D. (2007). *Using CBM for progress monitoring in reading.* Available *at studentprogress.org/summer_institute/2007/introreading/IntroReading_Manual_2007. pdf.*

Galvin, L. G. (2006). *Alphabet of space (Smithsonian alphabet book).* Norwalk, CT: Palm.

Gambrell, L. B. (2011). Seven rules of engagement: What's most important to know about motivation to read. *The Reading Teacher, 65*, 172–178.

Gannett, R. S. (2010). *My father's dragon: The bestselling children's story.* CreateSpace Independent Publishing Platform.

Garcia, E. G., Pearson, P. D., Taylor, B. M., Bauer, E. B., & Stahl, K. A. D. (2011). Socioconstructivist and political views on teachers' implementation of two types of reading comprehension approaches in low-income schools. *Theory into Practice, 50*, 149–156.

Gerber, C. (2013). *Seeds, bees, butterflies and more!: Poems for two voices.* New York: Henry Holt and Company.

Goldberg, W. (2008). *Sugar plum ballerinas: Plum fantastic.* New York: Disney Books.

Good, R. H. III, & Kaminski, R. A. (2002). *Dynamic Indicators of Basic Early Literacy Skills* (6th ed.). Eugene, OR: Institute for the Development of Educational Achievement. Retrieved November 30, 2009, from *dibels.uoregon.edu*

Grimes, N. (2009). *Rich: A Dyamonde Daniel book.* New York: Putnam Juvenile.

Gutman, D. (2004). *My weird school #1: Miss Daisy is crazy!* New York: HarperCollins.

Halladay, J. (2012). Revisiting key assumptions of the reading level framework. *The Reading Teacher, 66*(1), 53–62.

Hamilton, C. E., & Schwanenflugel, P. J. (2011). *PAVEd for Success: Building vocabulary and language development in young learners.* Baltimore: Brookes.

Hasbrouck, J., & Tindal, G. A. (2006). Oral reading fluency norms: A valuable assessment tool for reading teachers. *The Reading Teacher, 59*, 636–644.

Hayes, L., & Flanigan, K. (2014). *Developing word recognition.* New York: Guilford Press.

Heckelman, R. G. (1969). A neurological-impress method of remedial-reading instruction. *Academic Therapy Quarterly, 4*, 277–282.

Heckelman, R. G. (1986). N.I.M. revisited. *Academic Therapy, 21*, 411–420.

Hiebert, E. H. (2002). Standards, assessments and text difficulty. In A. E. Farstrup & S. J. Samuels (Eds.), *What research has to say about reading instruction* (pp. 337–369). Newark, DE: International Reading Association.

Hiebert, E. H. (2010, February). *Changing readers, changing texts: 1960–2010.* Jeanne Chall Memorial Lecture at Harvard University, Cambridge, MA.

Hiebert, E. H., & Martin, L. A. (2009). Opportunity to read: A critical but neglected construct in reading instruction. In E. H. Hiebert (Ed.), *Reading more, reading better* (pp. 3–29). New York: Guilford Press.

Hirsch, E. D. (2003, Spring). Reading comprehension requires knowledge—of words and the world. *American Educator*, pp. 10–13, 16–22, 28–30.

Hirsch, E. D., & Pondiscio, R. (2010–2011). There's no such thing as a reading test. *America Educator*, pp. 50–51.

Hoberman, M. A. (2006). *You read to me, I'll read to you: Very short stories to read together.* New York: Little, Brown.

Hoberman, M. A. (2009). *You read to me, I'll read to you: Very short scary tales to read together.* New York: Little, Brown.

Hoberman, M. A. (2012). *You read to me, I'll read to you: Very short fairy tales to read together.* New York: Little, Brown.

Hoberman, M. A. (2012). *You read to me, I'll read to you: Very short Mother Goose tales to read together.* New York: Little, Brown.

Hoberman, M. A. (2013). *You read to me, I'll read to you: Very short fables to read together.* New York: Little, Brown.

Hoberman, M. A. (2014). *You read to me, I'll read to you: Very short tall tales to read together.* New York: Little, Brown.

Hoffman, J. V. (1987). Rethinking the role of oral reading in basal instruction. *Elementary School Journal, 87,* 367–373.

Hoffman, J. V., & Crone, S. (1985). The oral recitation lesson: A research-derived strategy for reading basal texts. In J. A. Niles & R. V. Lalik (Eds.), *Issues in literacy: A research perspective* (34th yearbook of the National Reading Conference, pp. 76–83). Rochester, NY: National Reading Conference.

Holdaway, D. (1979). *The foundations of literacy.* Portsmouth, NH: Heinemann.

Hollingsworth, P. (1978). An experimental approach to the impress method of teaching reading. *The Reading Teacher, 31,* 624–626.

Howard, E. F. (1995). *Aunt Flossie's hats (and crab cakes later).* New York: Clarion Books.

Hunter, E. (2004). *Into the wild (Warriors, Book 1).* New York: HarperCollins.

Johns, J. (2012). *Basic reading inventory: Pre-primer through grade twelve and early literacy assessments* (11th ed.). Dubuque, IA: Kendall Hunt.

Juel, C., & Roper/Schneider, D. (1985). The influence of basal readers on first grade reading. *Reading Research Quarterly, 20,* 134–152.

Keats, E. J. (1964). *Whistle for Willie.* New York: Puffin Books.

Keats, E. J. (1976). *The snowy day.* New York: Puffin Books.

Kinney, J. (2007). *Diary of a wimpy kid.* New York: Amulet Books.

Kletzien, S., & Dreher, M. (2004). *Informational text in K–3 classrooms: Helping children read and write* (pp. 45–54). Newark, DE: International Reading Association.

Knowlton, J. (1985). *Maps and globes.* New York: HarperCollins.

Koskinen, P. S., & Blum, I. H. (1984). Repeated oral reading and the acquisition of fluency. In J. A. Niles & L. A. Harris (Eds.), *Changing perspectives on research in reading/language processing and instruction: Thirty-third yearbook of the National Reading Conference* (pp. 183–187). Rochester, NY: National Reading Conference.

Koskinen, P. S., & Blum, I. H. (1986). Paired repeated reading: A classroom strategy for developing fluent reading. *The Reading Teacher, 40,* 70–75.

Kostewicz, D. E., & Kubina, R. M. (2010). A comparison of two reading fluency methods: Repeated readings to a fluency criterion and interval sprinting. *Reading Improvement, 47*(1), 43–63.

Kuhn, M. R. (2004–2005). Helping students become accurate, expressive readers: Fluency instruction for small groups. *The Reading Teacher, 58,* 338–344.

Kuhn, M. R. (2009). *The hows and whys of fluency instruction.* Boston: Allyn & Bacon.

Kuhn, M. R. (2014). What's really wrong with round robin reading? *Reading Today Online.* Available at *www.reading.org/readingtoday/research#u34n5s-vp38.*

Kuhn, M. R., Ash, G. E., & Gregory, M. (2012). Battling on two fronts: Creating effective oral reading instruction. In T. Rasinski, C. Blachowicz, & K. Lams (Eds.), *Fluency instruction: Research-based best practices* (pp. 141–155). New York: Guilford Press.

Kuhn, M. R., & Schwanenflugel, P. J. (2006). Fluency-oriented reading instruction: A merging of theory and practice. In K. A. D. Stahl & M. C. McKenna (Eds.), *Reading research at work: Foundations of effective practice* (pp. 205–213). New York: Guilford Press.

Kuhn, M. R., & Schwanenflugel, P. J. (2007, May). *Time, engagement, and support: Lessons from a five-year fluency intervention.* Paper presented at the International Reading Association Preconference Institute No. 6, Toronto, Ontario, Canada.

Kuhn, M. R., & Schwanenflugel, P. J. (Eds.). (2008). *Fluency in the classroom.* New York: Guilford Press.

Kuhn, M. R., Schwanenflugel, P. J., & Meisinger, E. B. (2010). Aligning theory and assessment of reading fluency: Automaticity, prosody, and definitions of fluency. *Reading Research Quarterly, 45,* 232–253.

Kuhn, M. R., Schwanenflugel, P. J., Morris, R. D., Sevcik, R. A., Bradley, B. A., & Stahl, S. A. (2006). Teaching children to become fluent and automatic readers. *Journal of Literacy Research, 38,* 357–387.

Kuhn, M. R., & Stahl, S. (2003). Fluency: A review of developmental and remedial practices. *Journal of Educational Psychology, 95,* 3–21.

Labbo, L. D. (2005). From morning message to digital morning message: Moving from the tried and true to the new. *The Reading Teacher, 58,* 782–785.

Labbo, L. D., & Teale, W. H. (1990). Cross-age reading: A strategy for helping poor readers. *The Reading Teacher, 43,* 362–369.

LaBerge, D., & Samuels, S. J. (1974). Toward a theory of automatic information processing in reading. *Cognitive Psychology, 6,* 293–323.

Leslie, L., & Caldwell, J. (1995). *Qualitative Reading Inventory–II.* Boston: Longman.

Leslie, L., & Caldwell, J. (2010). *Qualitative Reading Inventory–5.* Boston: Pearson.

Logan, G. D. (1997). Automaticity and reading: Perspectives from the instance theory of automaticity. *Reading and Writing Quarterly: Overcoming Learning Difficulties, 13,* 123–146.

Madelaine, A., & Wheldall, K. (1999). Curriculum-based measurement of reading: A critical review. *International Journal of Disability, Development and Education, 46*(1), 71–85.

Madelaine, A., & Wheldall, K. (2004). Curriculum-based measurement of reading: Recent advances. *International Journal of Disability Development and Education, 51*(1), 57–82.

Marshall, J. (1974). *George and Martha.* New York: Houghton Mifflin.

McDonald, M. (2010). *Judy Moody was in a mood.* Somerville, MA: Candlewick Press.

McDonald, M. (2013). *Stink: The incredible shrinking kid.* Somerville, MA: Candlewick Press.

McKenna, M. C., Labbo, L. D., Conradi, K., & Baxter, J. (2011). Effective uses of technology in literacy instruction. In L. M. Morrow & L. B. Gambrell (Eds.), *Best practices in literacy instruction* (4th ed., pp. 361–394). New York: Guilford Press.

McKenna, M. C., & Stahl, K. A. D. (2009). *Assessment for reading instruction.* New York: Guilford Press.

McKeown, M. G., Beck, I., & Blake, R. G. K. (2009). Rethinking reading comprehension instruction: A comparison of instruction for strategies and content approaches. *Reading Research Quarterly, 44,* 218–253.

Meisinger, E. B., & Bradley, B. A. (2008). Classroom practices for supporting fluency development. In M. R. Kuhn & P. J. Schwanenflugel (Eds.), *Fluency in the classroom* (pp. 36–54). New York: Guilford Press.

Mesmer, H. A. E., Mesmer, E., & Jones, J. (2014). *Reading intervention in the primary grades: A common sense guide to RTI.* New York: Guilford Press.

Miller, J., & Schwanenflugel, P. J. (2006). Prosody of syntactically complex sentences in the oral reading of young children. *Journal of Educational Psychology, 98,* 839–853.

Minarik, E. H. (1978). *Little Bear.* New York: HarperTrophy.

Morris, D., & Nelson, L. (1992). Supported oral reading with low achieving second graders. *Reading Research and Instruction, 32,* 49–63.

Mostow, J., & Beck, J. (2005, June). *Micro-analysis of fluency gains in a reading tutor that listens.* Paper presented at the meeting of the Society for the Scientific Study of Reading, Toronto, Ontario, Canada.

Musti-Rao, S., Hawkins, R. O., & Barkley, E. A. (2009). Effects of repeated reading on the oral reading fluency of urban fourth-grade students: Implications for practice. *Preventing School Failure, 54*(1), 12–23.

National Assessment of Educational Progress. (1995). NAEP's Oral Reading Fluency Scale. *Listening to Children Read Aloud, 15.* Washington, DC: U.S. Department of Education, National Center for Education Statistics.

National Institute of Child Health and Human Development. (2000). *Teaching children to read: An evidence-based assessment of the scientific research literature on reading and its implications for reading instruction* (NIH Publication No. 00-4769). Washington, DC: U.S. Government Printing Office.

Neuman, S. B., & Celano, D. C. (2012). *Giving our children a fighting chance: Poverty, literacy, and the development of informational capital.* New York: Teachers College Press.

Osborne, M. P. (1992). *Dinosaurs before dark.* New York: Random House.

O'Shea, L. J., Sindelar, P. T., & O'Shea, D. (1985). The effects of repeated readings and attentional cues on reading fluency and comprehension. *Journal of Reading Behavior, 17,* 129–142.

O'Shea, L. J., Sindelar, P. T., & O'Shea, D. (1987). The effects of repeated readings and attentional cues on the reading fluency and comprehension of learning disabled readers. *Learning Disabilities Research, 2*(2), 103–109.

Palincsar, A. S., & Brown, A. L. (1986). Interactive teaching to promote independent learning from text. *The Reading Teacher, 39,* 771–777.

Pallotta, J. (1986). *The ocean alphabet book.* Watertown, MA: Charlesbridge.

Pappas, T. (1993). *Math talk: Mathematical ideas in poems for two voices.* San Carlos, CA: Wide World Publishing/Tetra.

Paris, S. G. (2005). Reinterpreting the development of reading skills. *Reading Research Quarterly, 40*(2), 184–202.

Paris, S. G. (2008, December). *Constrained skills—So what?* Oscar Causey Address presented at the National Reading Conference, Orlando, FL.

Park, B. (1992). *Junie B. Jones and the stupid smelly bus.* New York: Random House.

Pearson, P. D., & Gallagher, M. C. (1983). The instruction of reading comprehension. *Contemporary Educational Psychology, 8*(3), 317–344.

Prensky, M. (2001). Digital natives, digital immigrants, Part 1. *On the Horizon, 9*(1), 3–6.

Rasinski, T. V. (1989). Fluency for everyone: Incorporating fluency instruction in the classroom. *The Reading Teacher, 42,* 690–693.

Rasinski, T. V. (2004a). *Putting fluency research into practice.* Paper presented at the Preconference Institute No. 7 of the International Reading Association, Reno, NV.

Rasinski, T. V. (2004b). *Assessing reading fluency.* Honolulu, HI: Pacific Resources for Education and Learning. Available at *www.prel.org/products/re_/assessing-fluency.htm.*

Rasinski, T. V., & Hoffman, J. V. (2003). Oral reading in the school literacy curriculum. *Reading Research Quarterly, 38*(4), 510–522.

Rasinski, T. V., Padak, N., Linek, W., & Sturtevant, E. (1994). Effects of fluency development on urban second-grade readers. *Journal of Educational Research, 87,* 158–165.

Reutzel, D. R. (2003). Organizing effective literacy instruction: Grouping strategies and instructional routines. In L. M. Morrow, L. B. Gambrell, & M. Pressley (Eds.), *Best practices in literacy instruction* (2nd ed., pp. 241–267). New York: Guilford Press.

Reutzel, D. R., & Hollingsworth, P. M. (1993). Effects of fluency training on second graders' reading comprehension. *Journal of Educational Research, 86*, 325–331.

Reutzel, D. R., Hollingsworth, P. M., & Eldridge, L. (1994). Oral reading instruction: The impact on student reading comprehension. *Reading Research Quarterly, 29*, 40–62.

Reutzel, D. R., Jones, C. D., Fawson, P. C., & Smith, J. A. (2008). Scaffolded silent reading: A complement to guided repeated oral reading that works! *The Reading Teacher, 62*, 194–207.

Rey, H. A. (1973). *Curious George.* New York: Houghton Mifflin.

Roy, R. (1997). *The absent author (A to Z Mysteries).* New York: Random House.

Russell, R. R. (2009). *Dork diaries: Tales from a not-so-fabulous life.* New York: Aladdin.

Rylant, C. (1996). *Henry and Mudge.* New York: Aladdin.

Samuels, S. J. (1979). The method of repeated readings. *The Reading Teacher, 32*, 403–408.

Samuels, S. J. (2004). Toward a theory of automatic information processing in reading, revisited. In R. Ruddell & N. Unrau (Eds.), *Theoretical models and processes of reading* (5th ed., pp. 1127–1148). Newark, DE: International Reading Association.

Samuels, S. J. (2007). The DIBELS tests: Is speed of barking at print what we mean by reading fluency? *Reading Research Quarterly, 42*, 563–566.

Sanders, N. I. (2009). *D is for drinking gourd: An African American alphabet.* Ann Arbor, MI: Sleeping Bear Press.

Schulman, J. (2001). *You read to me and I'll read to you: Stories to share from the 20th century.* New York: Random House.

Scieszka, J. (2004). *The knights of the kitchen table (The Time Warp Trio #1).* New York: Puffin.

Shinn, M. R., & Shinn, M. M. (2002). *AIMSweb training workbook: Administration and scoring of reading maze for use in general outcome measurement.* Eden Prairie, MN: Edformation.

Silverman, R. D., & Meyer, A. G. (2014). *Developing vocabulary and oral language in young children.* New York: Guilford Press.

Snow, C. E., Burns, M. S., & Griffin, P. (1998). *Preventing reading failure in young children.* Washington, DC: National Academy Press.

Spache, G. D. (1981). *Diagnostic Reading Scales.* Monterey, CA: CTB: McGraw Hill.

Stahl, K. A. D. (2012). Complex text or frustration-level text: Using shared reading to bridge the difference. *The Reading Teacher, 66*, 47–51.

Stahl, K. A. D., & Garcia, G. E. (in press). *Developing reading comprehension: Effective instruction for all students in prek–2.* New York: Guilford Press.

Stahl, S. A. (1992). Saying the "p" word: Nine guidelines for exemplary phonics instruction. *The Reading Teacher, 45*, 618–625.

Stahl, S. A., & Heubach, K. M. (2005). Fluency-oriented reading instruction. *Journal of Literacy Research, 37*, 25–60.

Stanovich, K. E. (1986). Matthew effects in reading: Some consequences of individual differences in the acquisition of literacy. *Reading Research Quarterly, 21*(4), 360–407.

Stauffer, R. G. (1971). Slave, puppet or teacher? *The Reading Teacher, 25*, 24–29.

Stilton, G. (2004). *Lost treasure of the emerald eye.* New York: Scholastic.

Strickland, D. S., Ganske, K., & Monroe, J. K. (2002). *Supporting struggling readers and writers: Strategies for classroom interventions, 3–6.* Portland, ME: Stenhouse Publishers and Newark, DE: International Reading Association.

Taffe, S. W., & Bauer, L. B. (2013). Digital literacy. In B. M. Taylor & N. K. Duke (Eds.), *Handbook of effective literacy instruction: Research-based practice K–8* (pp. 162–188). New York: Guilford Press.

Thomson, M. (2009). *Keena Ford and the second-grade mix-up*. New York: Puffin.

Trachtenburg, P. (1990). Using children's literature to enhance phonics instruction. *The Reading Teacher, 43*, 648–654.

Truss, L. (2003). *Eats, shoots and leaves: The zero tolerance approach to punctuation*. New York: Gotham Books.

Vernon, U. (2012). *Dragonbreath*. New York: Puffin.

Walpole, S., & McKenna, M. C. (2009). *How to plan differentiated reading instruction: Resources for grades K–3*. New York: Guilford Press.

Wayans, K. & Knotts, K. (2008). *All mixed up! (Amy Hodgepodge #1)*. New York: Grosset & Dunlap.

Weiss, D. S. (1983). The effects of text segmentation on children's reading comprehension. *Discourse Processes, 6*(1), 77–89.

Williams, J. A. (2005). *Why is it snowing?* Berkeley Heights, NJ: Enslow.

Williams, V. B. (2007). *A chair for my mother*. New York: Greenwillow Books.

Yolen, J. (1996). *Commander Toad in space*. New York: Penguin Putnam.

Zion, G. (2006). *Harry the dirty dog*. New York: HarperCollins.

Index

An *f* following a page number indicates a figure; *t* following a page number indicates a table.